THE WORLD CHRIST KNEW

GUILD BOOKS No. 229

THE
WORLD CHRIST KNEW

The Social, Personal and Political Conditions
of His Time

By

ANTHONY C. DEANE

Canon of Windsor and Chaplain to H.M. The King

Published for

THE BRITISH PUBLISHERS GUILD

by Eyre & Spottiswoode, London

First published February, 1944
Reprinted April, 1944
First issued in this Edition, 1946

PRINTED IN GREAT BRITAIN BY
HAZELL, WATSON AND VINEY, LTD., LONDON AND AYLESBURY

PREFACE

In 1930, at Archbishop Lang's request, I lectured to the clergy of the Canterbury diocese on the background of the Gospels, and in the following year the three lectures appeared as a book, entitled *When Christ Came*. This has been out of print for some time. When the publishers suggested a new and revised edition, I decided not merely to revise but to recast and rewrite, in the hope of making the book useful to a wider public. Lectures addressed to a purely clerical audience had, naturally enough, a special character; they assumed, for example, a knowledge of New Testament Greek, they discussed the judicious use of the Gospel background in sermons, and in fact were written from a more or less professional point of view.

In its changed and enlarged form the book is meant for the general reader. The standard works on its subject, of which something is said in the final chapter, are voluminous, being based on full studies of rabbinic literature. They are apt to be unattractive in style; they are, indeed, valuable works of reference for the student rather than books for the ordinary man to read through. Popular works exist on special departments of the general subject, but I have not met a small book giving the average layman what I hope he may welcome—an outline picture of the Gospel background as a whole, so that he may realize the religious, economic and social outlook of the people among whom our Lord lived and taught. Without some such knowledge, the New Testament must often be misinterpreted; and however inadequately this attempt meets the average man's need, I am sure that the need is real.

A. C. D.

CONTENTS

CHAPTER ONE

THE GALILEAN

I

ELDERLY people may still remember the "Picture Bibles" with which they were presented in youthful days. The artists who illustrated these works did not lack imagination; the scenery and buildings they depicted were not to be found in any age within Palestine; the very odd costumes with which they clothed biblical personages were never worn in eastern lands or perhaps in any others. But the pictures did not lack vigour; some of us recollect, for example, the "Return of the Spies from the Promised Land"—two spies, staggering under the weight of a pole between their shoulders, from which hung a gigantic bunch of grapes, each about the size of a man's head.

At a later date there were illustrated Bibles of a more realistic quality, such as Tissot's, based upon long residence and careful observation in the Holy Land. In modern times large numbers of people have themselves made the pilgrimage to Palestine. Those who have not are able to learn from first-rate photographs what this country is like to-day, while skilful antiquarian reconstructions give them a sufficiently accurate idea of what it was like in the Gospel age. In one way and another, then, the physical and material setting of our Lord's earthly life are fairly well known. But what of the other, the invisible background? We have been made familiar with the kind of scenery in which our Lord's contemporaries lived, with the appearance of their towns and villages and even of the garments they wore. But can it be said that we are as well acquainted with the factors which shaped their thought—with their religious and political beliefs, their social and economic conditions? Sometimes this is supposed to be a subject which can be left to the expert, one which has no particular interest or importance for the ordinary Bible-reader.

Yet it matters to him immensely. If we are to understand the Gospels, we must try to put ourselves by sympathetic understanding among the friends and neighbours of Jesus

Christ. Only by doing this can we see things from their point of view and grasp the reason of their various attitudes towards him, the meaning of what they did and said. We must know, so far as this is possible, what kind of people they were, what conditions shaped their lives and controlled their thought, what were their ideas and habits and daily anxieties. Also, which obviously is still more important, it is essential to know as much as possible of the Gospel background in order to interpret rightly the words of our Lord. We are apt to miss the whole point of a parable, or of his answer to some question, because we fail to relate what he said with the circumstances of the country and age in which he lived. He did not deliver abstract discourses to humanity at large. We may believe him to have been conscious that his words would be treasured and studied by far-off generations of disciples; perhaps this consciousness led him to put much of his teaching in the form of great principles, which no change of time or outward setting would invalidate. Yet if in one sense his doctrine was timeless, in another it was timely. It was shaped by the needs, the limitations and the mental habits of the people to whom at the moment he was speaking. The form in which we have it is due to the fact that he came as a Galilean at a particular moment in history, and that his first thought was for the special needs of the people whose daily life he shared. In short, the more we know of the world Christ lived in, the better shall we understand what he said.

II

He came as a Galilean. This may well be the starting-point of our study. Everyone knows that our Lord lived on earth as a Palestinian Jew, but by no means everyone realizes how profoundly his life was influenced by the special part of Palestine in which his home-town stood. There was a considerable difference in creed and outlook between the Jews of Palestine and the Jews "of the Dispersion," as they were called. These, far more numerous than the Palestinian Jews, had made their homes at various centres in Asia, North Africa and Europe. The language they spoke and wrote was the colloquial, unliterary Greek used in every country at this time. The Jews of Palestine, though many of them had been obliged to learn Greek for business purposes, spoke Aramaic among them-

selves, and when the Scripture had been read in the ancient
Hebrew at a synagogue service, an interpreter added an
Aramaic version so that the people might understand. The
beliefs and ethical code of Jews of the Dispersion had been influenced by foreign cults and philosophy as those of the
Palestinian Jews had not. At the moment, however, we are less
concerned with such differences, important though they are,
than with the divisions in Palestine itself.

That part which lay on the west of the Jordan contained, in
the time of Christ, three districts: Galilee in the north, Judaea
in the south, with Samaria between them. Samaria we can
disregard; the Jews thought of it as not belonging to the Holy
Land at all, but as an island of foreigners, presuming to copy
the Jewish religion and maintaining their own worship and
Passover feast in rivalry to those of the Temple. Therefore
"the Jews have no dealings with the Samaritans."

Though there was no fundamental difference of this kind,
and the Jews of Galilee joined those of Judaea in keeping the
great religious festivals at Jerusalem, there were yet many
points of contrast between the peoples of the north and south,
and also between the districts in which they lived. "Go north
if you want riches, go south if you want wisdom," said a Jewish
proverb. Galilee was a fertile land of fields and gardens, olive-
groves and vineyards, studded with busy and densely-popu-
lated towns. The inhabitants were of many races, and, in addition to the permanent residents, there was a large floating
population, including both Jews of the Dispersion and Gentiles,
who as merchants and traders came on business visits. The
Jewish Galileans were warm-hearted, impulsive, enthusiastic;
the Gospel portrait of Simon Peter sets the type vividly before
us.

Judaea was a territory of arid, infertile limestone; most of its
ancient cities were in decay, and some in ruins. But its rocky
slopes led upwards to Jerusalem, dominated by the Temple;
to every Jew the symbol of God's watchful care for his chosen
people. The Judaeans were by temperament haughty and
reserved; they only, in their opinion, were faithful to the
religious Law which brought Israel into covenant-relationship
with God. It is true that the Sadducees, the strongest force in
Jerusalem itself, based such religion as they had on the Law
alone, while the Pharisees ranked the "Tradition," or rabbini-

cal interpretations of the Law, as having even greater authority. The bitterness between Sadducee and Pharisee was intense. Yet both united in deriding the Galileans, who retained something of that religious liberalism, something of that sense of the need of personal relationship with God, which it had been the mission of the prophets to emphasize. "This people who knoweth not the Law is accursed," said the official voice of Jerusalem, and its attitude towards the Galileans was one of disdain. "Art thou also of Galilee?" was a sneer, and "out of Galilee ariseth no prophet," said the Judaeans—a taunt which met its answer on Palm Sunday, when the people of Jerusalem asked "who is this?" and the pilgrim-crowd from the north replied in triumph: "this is the prophet, Jesus, from Nazareth of Galilee!" Although Aramaic was the native-tongue of Jews in the north and south alike, those of the north spoke it with a special accent, so that Peter in Jerusalem was quickly recognized as a Galilean, "for thy speech betrayeth thee." In short, there were many and considerable differences between the Judaeans and the Galileans, and there was no love lost between them. Judaea regarded Galilee with open contempt; Galilee resented the arrogance of Judaea.

Clearly enough, then, the fact that our Lord was a Galilean is among the most important to be remembered when we study the Gospel story. All his apostles also were men of Galilee, with one exception—and that exception was his betrayer. "Iscariot," *Ish-Kerioth*, probably means "man of Kerioth," a Judaean town. That he is given this place-name (none of the others have an equivalent) by the evangelists is itself significant; it may have seemed to them to account in part for his awful deed. But how daring an experiment it was in choosing the twelve to include one Judaean with eleven Galileans! It was rather like bringing together for daily companionship one Lancastrian and eleven Devonians,—or, one might almost say, one man from Northern Ireland with eleven from Eire. Did our Lord wish to insist by this choice that his message was not for the people of one district alone? Did he hope that the transforming force of his love would demonstrate its power by welding together the men of Galilee and the man of Judaea? At least it was a magnificently bold venture; perhaps our Lord did not regret having made it, even when he foresaw its failure and the awful consequence to himself.

III

How, then, did the fact that he was a Galilean affect the work he had come to perform? In some ways, especially during the earlier period of his ministry, it was a great help. When the news of the Baptist's imprisonment made him return to the north country, that the preaching of repentance and the coming of God's kingdom might be continued, he found among his own countrymen a hearing which had apparently been denied him in Judaea. These Galileans were, as has been said, an impulsive, but warmhearted and receptive race. The ordinary people—farmers, labourers, fishermen, traders, housewives—with a sprinkling of the rich and learned, thronged to hear his words and to marvel both at his message and his deeds of healing. In those crowded days of early success his chief difficulty was to get free from this enthusiastic crowd for the spaces of solitude and prayer which he knew to be essential to spiritual strength. At times, as an evangelist records, the demands on him were so insistent that there was no leisure even for a hasty meal. Soon he began to make tours through Galilee, and wherever he went he was welcomed as a distinguished scribe, or religious teacher, and invited to preach in the local synagogue on the sabbath-day. "He went into their synagogues throughout all Galilee," writes Mark,[1] "preaching and casting out devils." No such method, no such opportunities of preaching in the synagogues would have been allowed him in the south country; the Temple authorities at Jerusalem would have seen to that. But, partly because he was a Galilean addressing Galileans, the initial stage of his public ministry proved a triumphant success. In each town and village this wonderful and wonder-working new rabbi was welcomed and honoured. Once, after a multitude had been fed, an attempt was made to crown him as king; a misguided move which increased the animosity of Herod, yet showed the height he had attained in popular favour among the people of

---

[1]Mark i. 39, so also Matthew iv. 23. In the parallel passage of Luke (iv. 44) the best manuscripts have "he was preaching in the synagogues of Judaea," though many and not unimportant MSS. have "Galilee." But "Judaea" was often used loosely to describe Palestine in general, instead of a special district in it. It seems clear that Luke used it in this wide sense in this passage, and that some copyists changed it to "Galilee," to prevent its being mistaken for the district-name.

the north. It encouraged our Lord to hope that there would be no breach between him and the national church, that indeed this church would become a powerful ally in carrying out the reformation of creed and conduct he desired. Accordingly, as long as possible he gave his message in the synagogues, believing they would become centres of influence for propagating his doctrines.

Even in Galilee, however, some opposition was certain to be provoked sooner or later when results so striking as he achieved were due to so novel a teaching. When it came, it was from various sources. There was the political opposition of Herod Antipas, the Rome-appointed ruler of Galilee. He was unpopular, and in constant dread of plots to eject him from his post. He suspected such a plot when he heard that the Baptist was proclaiming the approach of some new "kingdom," and John's arrest followed. Now reports reached him that similar talk of a new kingdom was being heard from a new teacher, one Jesus of Nazareth, who indeed went further than John by claiming supernatural powers. Again therefore Herod, with his supporters the "Herodians," suspected treason. This feeling would be strengthened when news came that a considerable crowd of Galileans had attempted to make Jesus accept some sort of kingship.

Therefore while he remained in Herod's territory our Lord was in considerable danger. His disciples realized this, and took what precautions they could. They induced him to do much of his preaching on the beach of the Galilean lake, and had a boat in readiness, which sometimes he used as a pulpit. The reason is plain. If someone brought word that Herod's soldiers were in the neighbourhood and were coming to arrest Jesus, they would push off and take him across the lake to the other side. There he would be safe, for that further side of the lake belonged to the district governed by Philip, and therefore lay outside Herod's jurisdiction. There was a time when he seems to have been a fugitive from Herod, and had not where to lay his head. There was a considerable period which, for the sake of peace and safety, he spent in retirement outside Herod's territory. It was not that he feared death, but he must complete his mission before he died. "It cannot be that a prophet perish out of Jerusalem," was his message to "that fox," Herod Antipas.

Our Lord's initial success caused religious opposition also to develop. The guild, or fraternity, of the Pharisees had a good many members in Galilee. Of this fraternity more will be said in a later chapter; for the moment, we need remember only that its main purpose was to uphold the "Tradition," the rabbinic interpretation of the Law, as the code of conduct. The Pharisees in our Lord's audiences were genuinely shocked when they heard one whom they had accepted as a rabbi seeming to flout the Tradition and, in particular, violating its rules about the Sabbath. Sometimes they murmured their displeasure, or grumbled to the disciples; sometimes they expostulated openly. But they do not seem to have gone to the length of trying to exclude him from preaching in the synagogues. Much though at times they disliked his doctrine, they were conscious of his charm and power. Among them were thoughtful men, like Nicodemus, and it was a group of Pharisees who brought the friendly warning: "Get thee out, and go hence, for Herod would fain kill thee."

Far more dangerous religious opposition was brought into Galilee from the south—from Jerusalem, and the official heads of the national church. Travellers had given them news of an heretical teacher who was ensnaring the credulous folk of Galilee, those ignorant people who at no time paid due respect to the Law. The Jerusalem authorities sent scribes to Galilee, with orders to find out exactly what was happening, and to take such action as seemed to them necessary. These "scribes which came down from Jerusalem," as Mark terms them, were horrified by what they saw and heard, by the obviously immense hold upon the Galileans which Jesus had gained. As they could not deny that cures had been wrought, they asserted that these were due to the agency of evil spirits. And they told the rulers of the local synagogues, who dared not disregard orders with the weight of the Jerusalem authorities behind them, that this dangerous teacher must no longer be permitted the use of the synagogues for propagating his doctrine. The result was that this part of our Lord's ministry ended, and with it his hope of working through, and in harmony with, the national church in proclaiming his Gospel.

The official opposition, together with the perplexity which the new doctrine caused and some disappointment that he would not assume leadership as a political and economic reformer, detached from our Lord many who for a time had followed him. But the point to be specially noted is that the great mass of the Galileans were not influenced by these defections. When our Lord, after an interval, returned to their district, crowds of them gathered as before to listen to his teaching.

IV

And they were constant to the last. The Fourth Gospel makes specially clear the contrasting attitudes of Galileans and Judaeans towards Jesus. Writing when the separation of Christianity from Judaism had become complete, John usually employs the term "Jews" to describe the inhabitants of Judaea alone and in his account these Jews of Judaea are always hostile. "Jesus walked in Galilee," he says, "for he would not walk in Judaea, because the Jews sought to kill him." Of course our Lord had some friends in Jerusalem, just as he had some enemies in Galilee, yet, speaking generally, the Galileans were consistently his friends, the Judaeans increasingly his enemies.

With a vast concourse of pilgrims from the north, Jesus approached Jerusalem to keep the Passover and to announce himself as the Messiah. Near the entrance to the city, the Galileans formed a procession, and, with cries of "hosanna!" escorted Jesus through the gates in royal state. When preachers discourse on the fickleness of human nature, their favourite example is that the same people who had cried "hosanna" on Palm Sunday cried "crucify" on Good Friday. There is not a shred of evidence for this rather monstrous assertion, which traduces unjustly those loyal Galileans. They it was who cried "hosanna"; they who through the next three days successfully protected Jesus from arrest. They were the better able to do this because during the time of the Passover the pilgrims from the north in Jerusalem outnumbered the Judaean residents. The faithful Galileans were the "people" who thwarted the Jewish Council, until on the Thursday Iscariot's betrayal enabled it to seize our Lord under cover of darkness. Luke sets the story before us; on the Monday the enemies of Jesus were foiled; they "could not find what they might do, for all the people hung upon him, listening." On Tuesday, "the scribes and priests sought to lay hands on him in that very hour, and they feared the people." On the Wednesday, "the chief priests and scribes sought how they might put him to death, for they feared the people." It is absurd to suppose that only forty-eight hours later these same people, without any cause for the change, would shout "crucify him!" The rabble which did this was a very different crowd, made up of the numerous retinue employed by the Temple authorities with, likely enough, the dispossessed money-changers and live-stock traders. Most of them, perhaps, were hirelings from the dregs of the population, such as can easily be obtained at a low price in any oriental city.

In spite, then, of the frequent perplexity and occasional disappointment which he caused them, and although some of them fell away, it seems clear that the bulk of the Galileans revered and supported their great teacher and fellow-Galilean from beginning to end. They welcomed him with growing enthusiasm in the first stage of his ministry; in the last, they prolonged his life for several days, days in which the Sacrament of the Last Supper was instituted, and discourses, which have meant much to Christendom, were given.

The detailed story of our Lord's life and work on earth lies outside the scope of this book. What we are concerned with is the setting of that life and work, the Gospel background which must be taken into account if the Gospels themselves are to be rightly understood. What has been said in this chapter may help the reader to keep in mind the essential differences between Galilee and Judaea, and to realize that among the factors shaping our Lord's earthly life none was more powerful than that to his contemporaries he was Jesus of Nazareth, the Galilean.

CHAPTER TWO

A TROUBLED PEOPLE

I

By learning as much as we can of what the people in western Palestine thought, believed, hoped for and feared in our Lord's days, we shall understand better much of what he said to them, and realize also more clearly the difficulty of his task. Suppose, then, that in the year A.D. 30 we had been able to wander about Galilee and Judaea, staying both in towns and villages, having intimate talks with every class of inhabitant—leading rabbis, rulers of rural synagogues, rich landowners, small-holders, labourers, fishermen, women in their various homes, and slaves—what, at the end of the visit, would have been the impression we had received? What would have been our report on the Jews of Palestine as a whole?

The answer is not doubtful. We should have had to describe the atmosphere of Jewish Palestine as one of discontent, unrest, and more or less vague expectancy. Of course we should have to add that we had found numerous exceptions to a generalization of this kind. Very different moods and views will always exist among two million people; and that figure, or one slightly above it, seems to have represented approximately the population of Palestine at the time. In the course of our journey we should have come across individuals, families, and even large groups who were altogether content with the existing condition of things and in no way eager for change. One such group, for example, would be found in the Sadducean families in Jerusalem, whose influence was predominant on the national religious council, who controlled the Temple, and, by means of the dues and offerings exacted from the whole Jewish population, had become extremely rich. So long as the Temple system which brought them their wealth and influence was maintained, the subjugation of God's chosen people by the Roman Empire, odious to every devout and patriotic Jew, did not greatly concern them. They were even ready on occasion to declare publicly: "we have no king but

18

Caesar." What did perturb them, on the other hand, were reports from Galilee of a dangerous upstart whose teaching and practice were said to defy the Law, and therefore by implication to attack the system for which the Temple stood.

Elsewhere, too, we should have found a few wealthy people who were frankly indifferent to religion—like the rich man of the parable who "fared sumptuously every day," on fast-days and feast-days alike. They were quite satisfied with the existing order of things. Content of a very different kind we should have found in many sequestered homes, where the workers contrived to make enough for their daily needs, knowing little and caring less about public affairs. And there were devout folk, numerous enough to be classified as "the quiet in the land," who realized how evil the times were, yet were sure that God would intervene at his chosen moment to right them, and meanwhile were ready to wait in tranquil endurance.

Yet all these, however numerous and various, were exceptions; the general temper was one of discontent and unrest. We should soon have been made aware of this as we overheard murmured confidences between neighbours, shrill arguments in the market-places and, above all, discussion and interchange of news in the streets of Jerusalem at one of the great religious festival seasons. These brought together Jews from every part of Palestine and from oversea settlements, when rumours ran through the multitude and patriotic fervour mounted high. Looked at from almost any point of view, the national position was bad, and there was a widespread feeling —only too well justified by later developments—that it must become worse. Few of the counsels given by our Lord must have seemed more difficult to follow than that which urged his hearers not to be anxious about the morrow. They were oppressed by a growing economic problem; which for large numbers of them meant a fear that soon they would be unable to buy food. The economic problem was mingled, as always it is, with politics. There were labour difficulties and unemployment, with the crime and violence to which large-scale unemployment often leads. There were hopes that in some striking way God would rescue his people from their misfortunes. There were frequent rumours that a great national uprising was about to begin, and that a leader for it had been found. In short, the prevailing mood of the people among whom our Lord lived was tense, unsettled, unhappy.

II

To understand its effect upon our Lord's work it will be worth while to examine this background more closely. We will begin with the economic difficulty. While most people appreciate some of the political and religious problems of the Gospel period, the degree in which the financial factor was influencing every part of Jewish life in Palestine at this time, including even its religion, is less known by the average Bible-reader.

One source of the financial difficulties which afterwards became increasingly acute was the extravagance of Herod the Great. Having assisted the Romans to capture Jerusalem in 37 B.C. he was rewarded by being made ruler of Judaea and Samaria, with the title of king. From the first he was unpopular, partly because he was not himself a Jew but a native of Idumaea, the district adjoining Judaea on the south. Also he offended Jewish national and religious feeling by posing as an enthusiast for Hellenic culture and subsidizing it lavishly. His expenditure was always enormous, partly on bribes to Rome, in order to retain imperial favour, partly on luxuries for himself and his court, but most of all on gigantic building operations. He constructed cities and fortresses, he put up heathen shrines, and, in the hope of conciliating the Jews, he began the reconstruction of the Temple on a huge scale. This was continued long after his death, it was in progress throughout the years of our Lord's life on earth, and the disciples, it will be remembered, called his attention to its magnificence.

Herod's aim seemed to be to emulate Solomon, but Solomon was an independent king, not a mere vassal who had to pay heavily to an alien power for his right to rule. At first the Jews, little as they liked Herod personally, were dazzled by and admired his grandiose works. But the feeling disappeared when the bills began to come in and heavy taxation was levied in order to pay them. On Herod's death, in A.D. 4, the Jews complained to Rome that he had found their country rich and left it ruined. They asked that for the future a form of home rule might be allowed them. But Rome, after some hesitation, divided the territory among Herod's sons, though permitting none of them to be styled king. Antipas became tetrarch of Galilee, Philip of territory east of the Jordan and Archelaus ethnarch of Judaea, Samaria and Idumaea. Within a year the cruelties and tyranny of Archelaus had become intolerable. For once, Judaeans and Samaritans agreed; they combined to send another petition to Rome; "we will not have this man to reign over us" was their cry. If they might not be granted home rule, let a Roman procurator be put in charge. This was done, and Quirinus—whose name in the Authorized Version (Luke ii.) is given as Cyrenius—took office as the first procurator in A.D. 6.

The cause of his arrival should be noticed, because it refutes a rather common belief that the Jews bitterly resented the presence of a Roman governor in Jerusalem. No doubt the succession of procurators became increasingly unpopular as hatred of Rome increased, until, sixty years later, it caused the catastrophe of futile armed revolt. But the reason why Judaea had its procurator at the time of our Lord's birth was not that he had been forced by Rome upon an unwilling people but that the Judaeans had asked for him. They hoped that the authority of imperial Rome, upheld by armed force, would restore law and order. Tumults, robbery, assassination in the days of Archelaus had made life insecure and the conduct of business impossible. To a considerable extent, the hope of improvement was fulfilled. There were still occasional riots; it was still only too possible for a traveller from Jerusalem to Jericho to be attacked by highwaymen. Yet crime was now sternly repressed, and outwardly normal life in Palestine became peaceful enough.

III

But the installation in this way of direct Roman government had another result, less plainly foreseen and far less welcome. Rome did not protect its acquired provinces without charge. With the transfer to Roman jurisdiction of Jerusalem and the most important part of Palestine, a complete system of taxation was imposed, very much more onerous than the irregular tribute levied through Herod the Great. Now there was a poll-tax—without discrimination of sex or means, and payable annually—a water-tax, a city-tax, a road-tax, a house-tax, and others. In addition, there were import and export duties, with market tolls and payments levied when marketable commodities reached the gate of a town. Their burden was increased by the method employed for their collection. The Roman government saved itself trouble by farming out the payments, sometimes to the local procurator, more often to a syndicate of *publicani* in Rome. Their name was also given in common talk, though inaccurately, to the local collectors whom the *publicani* employed. Publicans in Rome and local agents in Palestine alike set themselves to make the utmost they could out of the business. It was honeycombed with knavery, and the men must have been few who, like Matthew and Zacchaeus, could master the temptations to dishonesty in such employment. These taxes and dues raised the price of almost all necessaries which the Jew wished to buy, and lessened the profit on anything he had to sell.

Yet, heavy though the burden was, there seems no reason for supposing that it was heavier in Palestine than in other outlying and conquered parts of the Roman Empire. Why, then, were its demands less tolerable in Palestine than elsewhere? Why was it resented, not merely on patriotic or religious grounds, but as causing immediate hardship and ultimate ruin?

The answer is clear when we recollect the unique character and constitution of the Jewish race. Other nations paid their domestic taxes chiefly in order to maintain standing armies. The Jews never had a standing army; they looked on themselves as a theocracy, under the special protection of God. They had a system of taxation, which in course of time had become heavy, but the proceeds were devoted to the maintenance of the Temple, its priests and its rulers. Therefore the punctual making of these payments was regarded as an essential religious duty—as, in fact, being made to God; a belief which the Temple authorities were careful to encourage.

When other nations were conquered by Rome, their armies ceased to exist, and with them the taxes for their maintenance. Instead, tribute had to be paid to Rome; yet, if this seemed a humiliating and lamentable change, probably the sums demanded were not much above those which had been required, while the country was still independent, to maintain its own armed force. The position of the Jews after conquest by Rome was very different. The taxes and dues they were required to pay in the name of their religion in no way diminished. Indeed, through a long period they had steadily increased. As Schürer (*Jewish People in the Time of Christ:* Div. II. Vol. i. 230) remarks: "The emoluments which the priests received from the people for their subsistence were, down to the time of the Exile, of a very modest and rather precarious kind. But subsequent to this latter period they were augmented almost beyond measure." The religious dues included the half-shekel payment to the Temple treasury, exacted from every Jew. There was tithe of crops and cattle, which the Pharisees extended even to garden herbs: "ye pay tithe of mint and anise and cummin," said our Lord. The first-fruit of crops, the first-born of animals, went to the priests, and an offering for the first-born child. Other dues were the sin-offering, the thank-offering, the shew-bread, contributions for the support of the poor and of local synagogues, with various "voluntary" offer-ings, which did not always deserve that name.

Yet, if there were a good deal of quiet grumbling at the increase of the religious taxes, and a growing dislike, especially in Galilee, of the Jerusalem hierarchy, we may still believe that the average devout Jew made these payments as an undoubted religious duty. Even when their total was considerable, it could have been supplied with little hardship if the religious taxes had stood alone. But they did not stand alone. And now we can realize why the Gospel period was one of financial stringency and discontent. The Jews were taxed twice over. They had to pay both their national religious taxes and the Roman civil taxes. Each demand was endurable by itself, but the two in conjunction were crushing.

Neither financial authority was in the least likely to mitigate its demands because of those made simultaneously by the other. Let us imagine that some anxious Jew carried his com-plaint to a friendly Roman official. Might not Caesar be willing to take less, he would ask, now that the religious taxes were so high? "That does not concern us," would be the answer. "You must make the best terms you can with your own reli-gious leaders—or evade their demands entirely, if you choose. We take no interest in that. But you are now living within the Roman Empire, you enjoy its protection, you benefit by the roads and bridges it has constructed for you—and naturally you must pay your tax in full. Any attempt to evade it would result in unpleasant consequences." After this rebuff, perhaps he would see what could be done with the Jerusalem hierarchy. To them he would protest that, much as he wished to contribute as before to the cause of religion, this had really become impracticable, by reason of what he was compelled to pay to Rome. The priests would raise their hands in horror. "Your suggestion amounts to blasphemy," they would reply. "It is not man but God whom you propose to rob. As for those odious Roman taxes, we shall—speaking unofficially—regard you as a patriot rather than a sinner if you can contrive to cheat the publicans. That, however, is your own affair. But any attempt to withhold your religious dues will not only cause you to be tried in our ecclesiastical courts but will bring upon you the wrath of God."

IV

Here, then, in this double taxation—Roman and Jewish, civil and religious—lay the chief cause of growing economic unrest. It had increased during the quarter-of-a-century that lay between the first arrival of a Roman procurator and the beginning of our Lord's public ministry. We can now appreciate the significance of two questions put to him; the first, through Peter, whether he sanctioned the payment of the Temple half-shekel; the other, whether he sanctioned the payment of tribute to Caesar. It was from the latter, no doubt, that the patriotic Jews longed to be set free. Over a long period attempts at rebellion against it were sporadic and quickly suppressed, though riots "at the time of the taxing" were ominous. Our Lord himself foresaw that the feeling of which such outbreaks were symptoms would increase as the years went by and the economic strain increased. At the end, because Jerusalem was blind to the supreme value to her of peace, there would follow a hopeless war with Rome, a siege of Jerusalem attended by unspeakable horrors, the capture and destruction of the sacred city.

But this tragedy lay forty years ahead. It is with the time of our Lord's ministry that we are concerned here. Two other factors which increased the financial stringency and consequent unrest should be mentioned. One was the rising cost and scarcity of food. The population, judged by modern standards, was small in relation with the area over which it was spread. Yet home resources were hardly adequate to supply its needs. Galilee had been, and in some districts still was, a fertile region, but its soil was shallow, with limestone beneath, so that the sower must beware of wasting his seed on rocky ground. And primitive methods of agriculture led, as in other Eastern lands, to soil exhaustion. The mountain slopes of Judaea produced little beyond vines, olives and figs. The fish taken in vast numbers from the Sea of Galilee was a great national asset. But the mass of the population was agricultural, and lived by sending to market the produce of its small-holdings. Inevitably the market and city tolls exacted by the Roman system raised prices, and diminished sales and profits. The duties on imported food made its cost prohibitive except to the wealthy.

Another trial afflicting the small-holder was the unfair competition he had to face owing to the employment of slave-labour by rich landowners. There were both Hebrew and "Canaanitish" slaves—those brought in from the districts of Tyre and Sidon. The small-holder, unable to purchase slaves, was obliged to hire labourers to assist him in his vineyard or garden, but when he brought his crops to market, they had to compete with what had been produced by slave labour, and consequently could be sold at a far lower price. Therefore many of the small agricultural holders were driven out of business, and those whom they had employed lost their jobs, "standing all the day idle in the market-place, because no man had hired them." And not a few of these unemployed resorted in despair to brigandage or other forms of crime. The bitterness of the extremely poor was intensified by the contrast of the few extremely rich people, both in Jerusalem and scattered over both Judaea and Galilee—though the larger number were in the southern district. Besides the wealthy Sadduceean families in Jerusalem, there were opulent merchants, bankers who made fortunes by extortionate usury, and landed proprietors able to purchase as many slaves as they required.

But the great mass of the people among whom our Lord moved stood between these extremes. Though very far from rich, they were not yet on the rocks of bankruptcy, though they feared that the tide of public affairs was carrying them rapidly in this direction. No wonder, then, that Palestine in those days was a land of unrest, or that the economic factor contributed largely to this disquiet. When we take it into account, we shall find that many passages in the Gospels grow luminous with new meaning. We will now see what hopes there were to offset the fears, and what was the attitude of our Lord himself towards that financial problem, closely intertwined with questions of politics and religious faith, which weighed so heavily on the people to whom his message was delivered.

CHAPTER THREE

STONES INTO BREAD?

I

THE period of our Lord's ministry was about halfway between the beginning of heavy and systematic taxation by Rome—preluded by a census to make sure that none should evade its demands—and the time when it reached a height which drove the Jews into desperate revolt. Yet, if the economic conditions were less crushing than they became subsequently, the times were already bad and seemed likely to become worse. Jesus came into touch with men and women of every class, but the majority of those among whom he worked were, like his own closest friends and neighbours, neither wealthy nor desperately poor. The rather widespread idea that he and his disciples had to endure great poverty is mistaken. It is derived from a single utterance of his at a special moment, a moment probably when he was being pursued from place to place by Herod's officers, and had not where to lay his head. The deduction as to his normal manner of life is as false as it would be to imagine that he was wealthy because at other times he was a welcome guest at rich men's tables. The group of disciples who owned a little fishing-fleet at Capernaum had to work hard for their living, yet they could afford to employ "hired servants," and were far from indigent.

In short, people of their class, the class to which, humanly speaking, our Lord belonged, comprising masons and craftsmen, small farmers, traders, fishing-boat owners and the like—managed to keep going comfortably enough when times were good. But the trouble with them, as it is still with their modern successors in Eastern lands, was that they had no margin. It was a typical figure which our Lord drew in picturing the man who had not so much as a spare loaf in hand when the arrival of an unexpected guest upset his domestic arrangements. Typical also was the woman whose whole capital had been reduced to ten pieces of silver. The loss of one drachma—in value about a shilling—was a real disaster; its recovery meant so much that she must call in her neighbours to share her rejoicing. Even in the days before heavy Roman taxation, few of the small farmers, traders or fishermen had been able to put by any reserve. Perhaps it was the costly help of the money-lender, to be found in every Eastern town and village, which enabled them somehow to survive bad harvests, or a period of trade depression, or a long spell of weather stormy enough to make fishing impossible. Yet in the past the periods of financial stringency due to such causes had been transient, and it was possible, by one means or another, to struggle on until better conditions returned. Now, on the other hand, the only probable change seemed to be that a bad time would be followed by a worse. How, people wondered, was improvement to come? Onerous as the religious payments were, devout Jews, regarding them as payments to God, could not press for their reduction. There could be no hope that Rome would reduce the civil taxation; on the contrary, it seemed to grow heavier year by year.

Can we wonder, then, that the people among whom our Lord lived were, as a body, discontented, restless, anxious? If with this mood of theirs in our mind we study again our Lord's teaching, much of it will seem to have new force. We shall understand, for example, why no fewer than fourteen of the parables are concerned, directly or indirectly, with money, for he knew how large a place it had in their minds. We shall understand why he warned them against taking too much thought for the morrow. And we shall understand—as, possibly, we may not have done before—why the prayer he taught includes the petition: "Give us to-day to-morrow's bread"; which is now known to be the true meaning of a familiar sentence. The Greek word translated by "daily" in our Bibles occurs in both the Matthew and Luke versions of the Lord's Prayer, but nowhere else in the New Testament, and its precise significance remained uncertain until modern times. The discovery is a real gain, an enrichment of the Prayer. No less than before the sentence is a prayer for our bread, a recognition of the truth that we depend on God for the supply of our bodily needs. Yet it is also, and perhaps primarily, a prayer for peace of mind, for freedom from worry, made for ourselves and for all who are haunted by the fear of want. Nothing can safeguard us so effectively from being anxious about "the morrow" as the knowledge that enough to meet its needs is already in our hands, and for this reassuring knowledge, with the release it brings from anxiety, our Lord encouraged his hearers to pray in the words "Give us to-day to-morrow's bread."

II

It is a prayer "as well for the body as the soul," for spiritual no less than for material benefit. To realize the economic background, with the consequent disquiet, of our Lord's time is to become aware of one of the chief hindrances he met when proclaiming the kingdom of God. Few people will be disposed to give whole-hearted attention to religious teaching when they are desperately bothered over domestic finance. Those to whom our Lord spoke were preoccupied in this way, were anxious for the morrow, were wondering about its supplies, were "thorny ground," in which "the cares of this world" choked the growth of the seed. What they eagerly desired were promises which would justify the vague hopes that mingled with their fears. Such hopes were of various kinds. One point was common to them all. Clearly enough, the domination of Palestine by Rome, tolerable though at one time it had seemed for the sake of the order and security it was to establish, had now proved to be the source of increasing financial difficulties. How could it be ended?

One sect, known as "the Zealots," held that it could only be overthrown by the sword. Their fathers had revolted, with disastrous results, against Herod the Great, and they themselves were eager for open rebellion against Rome when an opportunity should come. Their numerical strength in our Lord's time is difficult to estimate. Anything like open organization among them would very promptly have been suppressed. They were individual militarists, trying quietly to gain converts to their view. It is a remarkable fact that one of the Apostles, Simon Zelotes, had apparently been for a time a member of this party. If he still retained any of its views, he must indeed have been astonished by the doctrine of the Sermon on the Mount.

But even the Zealots, after their ill-starred attempt in the days of Herod, did not propose to begin another armed rising at a moment of their own choice. Like most of their fellow-Jews, they expected that, sooner or later, some Divine manifestation would rescue God's people. Where they differed from the rest was in their conception of the form this would take. They anticipated it as the appearance of a divine leader who, like Judas Maccabaeus, would summon the nation to fight. With supernatural aid, the Romans would be overcome and slaughtered by the triumphant Jews, and then a golden age would follow.

But probably the number of Jews with whom the Messianic hope meant a longing for bloodthirsty vengeance was quite small. Among the rest it assumed various forms. With many, especially those who had been influenced by the Baptist's message, it was deeply religious. Judaism, as officially taught, no longer contented them; far more appealing was the call given by the prophets to personal consecration, to a life lived in direct relationship with God. On such a life, they believed, the coming Messiah would insist as a condition of entrance to the kingdom he would set up, and the Baptist's call to "repent, for the kingdom of God is at hand" was, in their view, one to which the nation should respond. Others, again, were moved chiefly by political feelings. It seemed to them monstrous that Israel should remain subject to a foreign power. They trusted that, without any necessity for armed conflict, the appearance of the looked-for Messiah would mean the immediate regaining of national independence.

Yet perhaps a religious revival or a political change was not uppermost in the thoughts of most people when they hoped for the speedy coming of the Messianic kingdom. These things counted in varying degrees, and indeed all but a few Jews desired the emancipation of their race from the sway of Rome. But the chief reason why they looked eagerly for the coming of a divine kingdom was that it would deliver them from their present troubles, would mean some manifestation of God's power which would usher in a time of peace, prosperity and plenty. In other words, the dismal economic background of the Gospel age more and more coloured the Messianic hopes.

III

The development of this influence is to be seen in the "apocalyptic" writings which began to appear when the latest of the Old Testament prophets had long passed away. The average Bible-reader does not always realize that an interval of something like four-and-a-half centuries separates Malachi from Matthew. The vogue of the writings known as "apocalyptic" began about 200 B.C. and continued until about A.D. 100; the Apocalypse of St. John being possibly the latest and certainly the greatest example. Of its religious influence on the thought of our Lord's age and the use he himself made of it something will be said in the next chapter. For the moment, we need only note its general character. It was written to bring encouragement in bad times, and this it did by visions of an approaching divine judgment, which would inaugurate a glorified life of happiness and prosperity. Sometimes the background of this new era was to be heaven, sometimes a transformed earth; often it is not easy to be sure which setting the writer means to describe. Some of the earlier apocalyptic books looked for the coming of a personal Messiah, human or divine —and this hope was revived by the teaching of the Baptist— but in the later books we find instead a more vague and general idea of a "theophany," or manifestation of God and his power

As apocalyptic was always meant to console for a bad present by pictures of a bright future, so when the main factor in the bad present was economic trouble, the main joy promised for the bright future was material prosperity. Starving travellers often tell how they feasted in their dreams, or beguiled tedious hours by planning the ample meals they would order on their return to civilization. Apocalyptic brought the same kind of vision before people suffering poverty and privation. Life in heaven was represented almost as an oriental banquet, and the chief feature of the new kingdom which God would establish was universal wealth with plenty to eat and drink. The merchant's city was to be magnificent, spacious, uncrowded. The countryman's land was to be miraculously fertile. So far from taxes being paid to any foreign power, all other races would humbly bring their offerings to Israel.

Indeed, it seems clear when we study both the small proportion of apocalyptic literature found in the Bible—inclusive of the Apocrypha—and the larger proportion outside it, that economic trouble had given the Messianic hope a special form, and one which made it specially welcome. But to say this is not to suggest that it was the only factor, and still less that the Messianic expectation originated in the prevailing desire for happier financial conditions. Some Jewish writers have attempted to explain away our Lord's success in Galilee by an argument of this kind. For example, Dr. Klausner in his *Jesus of Nazareth* (Eng. translation, p. 400) maintained that "if Jesus successfully taught of the kingdom of heaven, it was simply and solely because of the disordered condition of life in the country and the bad economic conditions generally." This is an untenable view. Belief in the coming of a divine kingdom had existed, and had been keenly cherished, long before the financial situation had deteriorated. It had begun as a religious aspiration, and in our Lord's time, as we have noted, there was still a definitely religious element in it, apart from the political and economic longings with which it had come to be linked. That the people among whom he lived were anxious and distressed over the financial situation and outlook is true enough. As we have noted, his work was hindered, not helped, by their absorption in such matters. Almost all were anxious, many were close to despair. It is essential to keep this picture of their restlessness before us if we are to gain an accurate idea of the Gospel background. We must remember also how powerful an influence rumour was—and indeed still is—among Eastern peoples. Stories of all kinds about the appearance of the awaited Messiah, about new decrees and new burdens which Rome was said to be contemplating, about risings reported to have broken out or to be imminent in this place and that, went from town to town, were keenly discussed in the market-place, increased yet further the disquiet of the people. Its main cause, as we have seen, was financial trouble due to food shortage, slave competition and, above all, dual taxation. But those who expected to hear from our Lord the promise of some speedy remedy for these growing ills were disappointed.

IV

This fact deserves close attention. The more clearly we know how important the economic problems of the day seemed to the audience our Lord addressed, the more we shall marvel at his resolute detachment from them. He had made his decision about this in the forty days of meditation and temptation which preceded the beginning of his ministry. In the narratives of both Matthew and Luke the temptation to change stones into bread comes first, and we may well suppose that of the three it was the most insidious, the most difficult to conquer. The tremendous force of the suggestion, which afterwards our Lord described in this picturesque form to his disciples, is easy to understand. Each of the three temptations represented what seemed like a short cut to gaining immense influence over the populace. With this hold upon them secured, he could give his spiritual teaching to multitudes who would then be ready to hear it. Had he yielded to the first temptation, he would have come forward as an economic and social reformer. He would have promised to supply the hungry with food, using his supernatural power not once or twice but frequently for this purpose. He would have claimed a hearing as about to lead a great popular movement against the fiscal exactions of Rome, the unfair distribution of wealth, and the competition of slave-labour. By such means he could have secured at once a large and enthusiastic following. "Command that these stones be made bread" was a temptation to take this easy course, with the suggestion that when popular favour had thereby been secured, the opportunity for proclaiming his Gospel to receptive ears would be ready-made.

He conquered the temptation. He stood consistently apart from the economic, social and political controversies of his time. When asked about the payment of religious dues to the Temple and of tribute to Caesar, he sanctioned both. Keenly though he sympathized with the trials of the poor, he regarded their compensations as so great that "blessedness"—and the word in the Beatitudes would be rendered more accurately by "happy" than by "blessed"—was not merely their future compensation but their present possession. He seemed to anticipate, and made no protest against, the indefinite survival of poverty; " the poor," he said, "ye have always with you."

He was keenly alive to the special dangers of wealth. A wealthy man whose character was being mastered by his riches should wholly abandon them. But the rich man who mastered his possessions and used them well was thereby training his character, and proving himself worthy to be trusted with the "true" riches, immaterial and imperishable. It was, in fact, character, the soul-life, which mattered; wealth and poverty were unimportant except so far as they impinged on character. He would be no judge or divider. He was intensely anxious for the conversion of sinners, and not at all for the inversion of institutions or the division of wealth.

Indeed, the apparent aloofness of our Lord from those social and economic issues which seemed to them of primary importance must often have perplexed, and at times provoked, the people among whom he lived. They have had a similar effect upon some of his modern interpreters. Their anxiety to find the highest sanction for their own doctrines and schemes of reform has urged them to find a social agitator and revolutionary in the Jesus Christ of the Gospels. If we feel ourselves free to question his divine wisdom, we may regret that he did not choose to develop his mission to the human race along such lines. What, on the other hand, we may not do is to ignore or to pervert the incontestable evidence of the four Gospels, to claim their authority for statements which they show to be false, to substitute an imaginative picture for their portrait of Christ. If their record is historic, then it is not a matter of opinion but a fact of history that our Lord consistently refused to entangle himself with current economic and social matters. He put forth no programme, announced no schemes of reform, although he could have commanded immense popularity by taking that course. He had indeed come to found a kingdom, and devoted a large share of his teaching to setting out its character, its principles, and the conditions of entry into it. But explicitly he said that his kingdom was not to be of this world; its basis was to be not political or economic but spiritual.

Must we then conclude that the economic difficulties which darkened the lives and filled the thoughts of his neighbours were of no concern to our Lord ? Must we believe that slavery, fraudulent oppression of the poor, and the many other social evils which he encountered daily seemed to him unimportant and needing no redress? To ask this question is to answer it. All that we know of Jesus Christ, the lover of mankind, infinitely wise, tender, sympathetic, makes it wholly incredible that he should not have desired to change conditions which brought suffering and unhappiness to the men and women he loved. But a further question then presents itself: why, then, did he make no perceptible effort to modify the economic and social order of his day? Why did he even seem to acquiesce— as undoubtedly he did seem—in the continuance of faulty systems? So far as his recorded utterances show, when directly challenged—as over the payment of religious and civil taxes— he accepted things as they were; at other times he appeared simply to ignore the burning questions of his day, as though for him their problems did not exist.

And this, in one sense, was profoundly true. He seldom glanced at them because his gaze was fixed steadily on something far more important. The solution of economic and social problems would come in due time as a by-product of the work he planned to accomplish, but in themselves they were merely external and almost negligible symptoms; he had set himself to cure the disease. Merely to allay the symptoms would be to leave the source of evil untouched, for that source was human sin. The one way, in his view, to reform human society was to transform the men and women who composed it. Outward change would have no value unless it were the product of inward change; what he designed was not a new setting out of which might emerge a new way of life, but a new way of life which, incidentally and ultimately, would lead to a new setting. "Reshape your economics," ardent reformers have urged, "provide model institutions, and you will be able to count on a supply of good citizens with a high standard of life." "Be, and lead others into becoming, my true disciples," is the counter-policy which our Lord sets forth; "put the knowledge and service of God first, build upon the rock of character, and those changes in the setting of life which you rightly desire will be added to you." The one method works from without, the other from within. The one invokes spiritual power to make man good, the other devises machinery to make him comfortable. It was the welfare of the soul which Christ put first, so that it might be brought into close relationship with God and be purified from evil; any other scheme for improvement seemed merely to cleanse the outside of the platter in a vague hope that the inside would somehow cleanse itself.

At a time when most people were eager for a deliverance of a special kind, it was not easy to teach them that the deliverance he offered was different, to be sought by different means, and that only when spiritual reform had been achieved would economic or social improvement of the right sort become possible. By every means, therefore, he would try to guard against any misunderstanding of his purpose and message. How quickly it might be misunderstood he had found when, by way of exception, he did minister to the crowd's bodily need, with the sequel that the enthusiastic multitude wished to make him king. "Ye seek me because of the loaves ye did eat," he complained afterwards.

We have found, then, an answer to our question. Our Lord deliberately stood apart from economic and social questions, he would even seem altogether indifferent to them, because any show of interest in them would have diverted the minds of his hearers from the teaching of supreme importance which he had come to give. A large popular following would have been welcome enough, but the price of gaining it—the price of being mistaken for a political leader, chiefly concerned with material prosperity and other affairs of this world—was one he would not pay. His decision meant turning back from an easy road to popular favour. But he had seen all the alluring possibilities of taking this road, he had realized how it would obscure his true purpose, he had made his final choice against it, when determining beforehand in the wilderness the methods by which his mission on earth was to be accomplished.

To realize the economic and political conditions in Palestine at the period of our Lord's ministry is to gain in many ways a better understanding of the Gospel narratives. It is also to understand better what temptations our Lord mastered and what difficulties he faced—an understanding that will intensify the awe and reverence we feel when we study the life on earth of the divine Master.

CHAPTER FOUR

THE PEOPLE'S RELIGION

I

WHEN our Lord began his work as a religious teacher, what foundation did he find on which he could build? What was the creed of Judaism as set forth by the ecclesiastical authorities at Jerusalem? How far did it coincide with the belief of the ordinary man or woman in Palestine? When Christ addressed the people who thronged to hear him, what could he assume to be their ideas about God, duty, sin, prayer, life after death? These, evidently enough, are not merely questions of antiquarian interest; to find the answers to them will help us greatly in understanding the Gospels. It will show us often the true meaning of what Christ said and the reason why he said it.

In one sense, the Palestinian Jews were the most religious nation that ever existed. In fact, they might be described as a church rather than a nation. Religion governed the whole of their lives, and they had hardly any interests outside it. They had no civil laws or government, apart from those imposed on them by Rome. The principal authority they recognized was not, to use modern terms, a Parliament but a Church Council—the high Sanhedrin at Jerusalem, and every town had its local Sanhedrin. They had no education other than religious education, no literature other than religious books, no culture, no music or art or oratory, other than those directly linked with religion. Except for such technical knowledge as was needed to earn a living, the range of their intellectual equipment was extraordinarily small.

This limitation was not found in anything like the same degree among the Jews "of the Dispersion," who had settled themselves permanently in other lands. Many of them could not even speak the Aramaic of the Palestinian Jews; Greek was their language, they learnt something of Greek culture, and the creed of Judaism as they held it was often modified by Greek philosophy. But it is with the Palestinian Jews, among whom Christ lived, that we are concerned here, and one of the

chief aims of the Pharisees, whose influence was stronger than
that of any other body, was to safeguard Judaism from Hellen-
ism. The line of reasoning which made them take this course
was simple. The Greeks were heathen, and many of the forms
of worship they practised were grossly immoral as well as
idolatrous. None of God's chosen people must run the risk of
contamination from this source, and therefore all acquaintance
with Greek thought, literature and art must be forbidden. No
doubt this veto was often disregarded among the Jews of the
Dispersion, but in Palestine it was accepted without question.

To understand the official creed of Judaism as it was taught
in our Lord's time we have to remember its earlier states. In a
striking degree the Israelites, unlike almost every other people,
had given their worship to one God alone. There had been
occasional lapses, when they were led astray by the nations
with whom, as conquerors or conquered, they had come into
close touch. Yet these defections were local and short-lived.
While worshipping one God, however, they did not in early
days deny the existence of others. Yahweh—the name represented by "Jehovah" in our English Bible—was the national
god of the Israelites. Other nations had their own guardian
deities, as Chemosh the god of the Moabites, Ashtoreth the
goddess of the Zidonians, Milchom—or Molech—the god of
the Ammonites. Each of these was recognized to be the protecting god of his own people, as Yahweh was the protecting
god of Israel. At this stage the Israelites did not question the
existence of other deities; what they did maintain was that
Yahweh excelled all the rest in power and wisdom. Even in the
Psalms this is, at times, the point of view, as in Psalms 86.8 and
89.6, which run, in the familiar Prayer-Book version: "Among
the gods there is none like unto thee, O Lord: there is not one
than can do as thou doest": "What is he among the gods that
shall be compared unto the Lord?" It was long before the
people were ready to accept such teaching as that given in
Isaiah xliv. 6: "I am the first and I am the last, and beside me
there is no God."

Yet by degrees this truth prevailed, and the people of Israel
not merely worshipped one God only, as before, but became
sure that no other gods existed. When this had once become
their accepted creed, they guarded their monotheism—their
belief in one God alone—with the most scrupulous care. They

became so anxious to deny the existence of any other super-natural power that they insisted on attributing every incident of human life, good and evil alike, to the one God. "Shall we receive good at the hand of God," they asked, "and shall we not receive evil?" "Shall evil befall a city and the Lord hath not done it?" writes Amos, the earliest of the prophets. When an evil spirit afflicts Saul, it is described as "an evil spirit from the Lord." Such a theory of course greatly complicated the problem of evil for the many thoughtful people who already were perplexed by it. How could evil proceed directly from the God who was perfect goodness? We shall find an interesting illustration of the way in which the need of an escape from this dilemma was felt when we compare two accounts, written at different times, of the same incident—David's numbering of the people. The story as we find it in 2 Samuel xxiv begins:

> And again the anger of the Lord was kindled against Israel, and he moved David against them to say, Go, number Israel.

Then David and the people are punished for what David has done—though this is what God moved him to do. To the compiler of Chronicles, writing centuries later, such a statement seemed intolerable, and accordingly when he re-wrote the story (1 Chronicles xxi), in his version it began:

> And Satan stood up against Israel, and provoked David to number Israel.

Between the times when these two books were written had come the period of Israel's captivity and exile in Babylon. When Babylon passed into Persian hands the close contact between Persians and Israelites had a considerable influence on the religion of Judaism, an influence which developed further in the post-Exilic age. In the Persian religion a large part was taken by angels and demons, by supernatural beings both good and bad. To some extent a parallel belief had existed from early days among the Israelites, but it assumed a far more prominent place in their thought after they had been in touch with Persian doctrine. It helped them to escape from two difficulties. As they wished to emphasize the supreme trans-cendence of the one God, they felt that he must not be sup-posed, like the pagan deities, to intervene directly in human affairs. Now they could believe that, with no loss of dignity, he communicated with the human race by means of messengers, his angels. Again, monotheism had no longer to be safeguarded by attributing everything, evil no less than good, to the one source. Without sharing the Persian "dualism"—for in that creed two rival divine powers existed, the one good, the other evil—the Israelites could at least be freed now from having to suppose that God was the source of temptation and of all human calamities. These could be ascribed to Satan and to the malignant supernatural beings under his command, and many forms of bodily and mental disease were attributed to "possession" of their victims by "devils." In apocalyptic literature the heavenly beings were classified under a hierarchic system, which was adopted in rabbinic teaching. Under it there were recognized ultimately three groups, each containing three orders: cherubim, seraphim, thrones; dominions, virtues, powers; principalities, archangels, angels. Representations of these "nine orders of angels" in carvings and painted windows are still to be found in ancient churches of our own country. St. Paul's references to some of these orders of heavenly beings will be remembered, and he described the powers of evil as forming similar cohorts; man's struggle, he wrote, is not with flesh and blood, but with evil principalities and powers, with spiritual hosts of wickedness.

Apart, however, from such details, the point to be remembered in reading the Gospels is that the Palestinian Jews of our Lord's time—except the Sadducees—were sure that mankind is surrounded by armies of supernatural beings, both good and bad. The world is full, they believed, of angels bringing messages from God (when, exceptionally, they might become visible to human eyes) and guarding from peril; and of demons who try to harm both soul and body, and to outwit the watchful protection given by the good angels. Belief in angels was amply confirmed by our Lord; only from his own words, for example, could the disciples have learnt that when he was solitary in the wilderness "angels came and ministered unto him." The belief is part of our Christian heritage, as the Feasts of the Annunciation and St. Michael remind us, yet for the average Christian of modern times it is far less vivid than in past ages, and seldom a factor influencing his daily life, as it certainly influenced the people among whom our Lord lived.

II

They—except again the Sadducees—believed in personal immortality also. The Old Testament references to what awaits man after death are various in their doctrine, and not a few of them are worded so obscurely that their precise meaning is uncertain. In their earliest days the Israelites, like every other primitive race, believed in some form of survival, and this belief was linked with magical rites and forms of worship which could not be combined with the pure worship of Jahweh. Instead, a belief seems to have developed in a gloomy form of underworld—"Sheol" was its name—in which mere phantoms of humanity survived. But if this were the most widespread and even, in a sense, the officially taught doctrine, individual departures from it are not rare in the Old Testament, ranging from a hopeless creed of annihilation to something like confidence in personal immortality. Those who know the Psalms will easily recall the very different views, written at different times and in different moods, which they contain on this subject. On the one hand, there is the infinitely dismal picture of Sheol in Psalm 88, when almost in derision the writer asks:

Dost thou shew wonders among the dead:
Or shall the dead rise up and praise thee?
Shall thy loving-kindness be shewed in the grave:
Or thy faithfulness in destruction?
Shall thy wondrous works be known in the dark:
And thy righteousness in the land where all things are forgotten?

—and, on the other, the glorious confidence of Psalm 73: "thou shalt guide me with thy counsel: and after that receive me with glory." These are but two of many contrasting examples. Detailed examination of this difficult subject clearly lies beyond the scope of these pages. What we need to observe is that at the end of the Old Testament period the average Jew believed only in some rather nebulous form of spirit-survival after death, whereas at the beginning of the New Testament he believed in personal immortality, in a resurrection, and in a Day of Judgment.

This helps us again to realize that the intervening centuries have to be taken into account, and that they saw an immense development in Jewish religious thought. Foreign influences no doubt did much to encourage belief in personal immortality, but in the last two centuries before the birth of Christ such belief was enshrined in and popularized further by apocalyptic writings. In the previous chapter something was said about the general character of this literature—literature with a "forward look," cheering people in bad times by visions of the glorious and triumphant future, of, as we should now say, the "new order," which God had in store for the faithful. Included in these visions were pictures of a Judgment Day in which sometimes God himself and sometimes a Messiah would appear as judge. Apocalyptic came when prophecy had long since been silenced, and its influence was vast. As if to show that they were not out of harmony with ancient traditions, these writings were linked with the names of great men of the past; among those which have survived, for example, are *The Book of Enoch, The Testaments of the Twelve Patriarchs, The Assumption of Moses, The Ascension of Isaiah.*

Unmistakable allusions to the apocalyptic writings abound in St. Paul's letters; in the Epistle of Jude there is a direct quotation from the Book of Enoch, and it is clear that apocalyptic literature—of which probably no more than a small proportion has come down to us—had a strong influence on the Jewish religion in New Testament times. It is of some importance for us to remember that when our Lord spoke of a Judgment Day and described its setting, he was not bringing unfamiliar ideas before his listeners. On the contrary, he borrowed the imagery of apocalyptic writings, and to keep this in mind will often save us from misinterpreting what he said. Here, for example, are some sentences (in Dr. Charles's translation) from chapter lxii of Enoch—a chapter of which about 150 B.C. is the probable date:

> And the Lord of Spirits seated him on the throne of his glory . . . and there shall stand up in that day all the kings and the mighty and the exalted and those who hold the earth, and they shall see and recognize how he sits on the throne of his glory, and righteousness is judged before him. And one portion shall look on the other, and they shall be terrified, and they shall be downcast of countenance . . . when they see that Son of man sitting on the throne of his glory. And he will deliver them to the angels for punishment, to execute judg-

ment on them . . . And the righteous and the elect shall be saved on that day, and they shall never thenceforward see the face of sinners and the unrighteous, and the Lord of spirits will abide over them, and with that Son of man shall they eat and lie down and rise up for ever and ever.

The likeness between this language and that of Matthew xxv is striking:

When the Son of man shall come in his glory, and all the angels with him, then shall he sit on the throne of his glory: and before him shall be gathered all the nations: and he shall separate them one from another, as the shepherd separateth the sheep from the goats: and he shall set the sheep on his right hand and the goats on the left . . . . And these shall go away into eternal punishment, but the righteous into eternal life.

III

So our view of the average Palestinian Jew's religion in our Lord's day begins to grow clear. He had an unquestioning faith in and worshipped the one God, whose relations with Gentile races were variously interpreted, but beyond all doubt was in a unique and special way the God and protector of his chosen people Israel. Fully as the Jew believed in angels, he never worshipped them—though at a later time, as St. Paul's Colossian letter shows, some Gentile Christians were tempted to do this. He looked for the coming of a Messiah, but beliefs about the form which the Messiah's work would take differed greatly, and increasingly the Messianic hope was coloured by the economic troubles of the time, so that escape from the dominion and taxation of Rome became the boon most eagerly anticipated. Israel would again become a pure theocracy, supreme among the kingdoms of this world. At the end there would be a Last Judgment, either preceded or followed by the resurrection of the dead, when the good would enjoy heavenly rapture and feasting as God's guests, while wicked men and evil spirits would be everlastingly punished.

For a formal creed, the Jew had the "*Shema*"—so named from its opening word, as creed is from *credo*—which was made up of three passages of Scripture, Deut. vi. 4–9, xi. 13–21, Num. xv. 37–41, placed in this order. The stately beginning is familiar; "Hear, O Israel; the Lord our God is one Lord, and thou shalt love the Lord thy God with all thine heart . . . ." (It will be noticed that Lev. xix. 18, "thou shalt love thy neighbour as thyself" was not included in the *Shema*). Then the Jew is exhorted to teach the divine commandments of the Law to his children, and to talk of them continually. The second passage promises abundant crops and harvests "if ye shall hearken diligently unto my commandments"; the concluding passage from Numbers orders the Jew's clothes to be fringed in a way that will remind him of the Law, and reiterates: "I am the Lord your God, which brought you out of the land of Egypt to be your God: I am the Lord your God." Every male Jew was expected to recite the *Shema* twice a day—no doubt some of the Pharisees made a point of doing this in public—and it was used also, together with certain prayers, at the beginning of each service in the synagogue.

The Law, and the "Tradition" which applied and amplified it, formed indeed the basis of Pharisaic Judaism, which was the official creed of most of Palestine at this time. The Law, it was believed, represented a kind of covenant between Yahweh and the people of Israel. In its earliest and crudest form, this meant that they, on their part, promised to worship Yahweh alone as their national God, and to obey in every detail the code of law and morals given by Yahweh to Moses as their representative. On the other part, Yahweh undertook, so long as they obeyed the Law, to show that he was more powerful than any other national god, to enable Israel to conquer their enemies, and to give them material prosperity.

None the less the Law, when rightly interpreted and followed, set a noble and lofty standard, free from mere formalism, and demanding a deeply religious personal relationship with God. To see how rich the Law could be in spiritual suggestiveness to a devout Jew we have only to look at the 119th Psalm, every verse of which meditates on some aspect of the Law as God's "word," "statutes," "testimonies," "judgments," and so forth. But by degrees as the Law was elaborated into a more comprehensive and artificial code, truly spiritual devotion was replaced by that respect for its mere letter which is conveniently described as "legalism." Legalism made the Law an end, instead of a means. In the earlier stage, observance of the Law had been valued as a help to a good life, a life of inward holiness, of clean hands and a pure heart. But when legalism prevailed, keeping the Law became, in effect, all that mattered, and those who kept it were the "righteous." This interpretation destroyed the moral sense, and its prevalence was one of the chief obstacles which our Lord had to encounter.

IV

He had to restore its real meaning to "righteousness." The ordinary man knew that for him exact compliance with the Law as amplified by rabbinical tradition was impossible; this righteousness was within the reach only of the Pharisees and their scribes. Imagine, then, his surprise when he was told that his righteousness must exceed that of the scribes and Pharisees if he were to enter the kingdom of God! He had been taught that if he rubbed corn in his hands on the Sabbath, or failed to wash his drinking-cup according to the prescribed method, he was a sinner. But he did not cease to be righteous if he played a mean trick on a neighbour, provided he could do it by some device which did not technically infringe the Law. Our Lord described one subterfuge of this discreditable kind. By the Law a man was bound to maintain his parents when they became old and necessitous. But suppose he wished to escape this obligation? Then he would go through the form of making over his possessions to the Temple authorities, with an understanding that later—less a fee for this service—they should be restored to him. His parents, compelled by extreme want, would sue him in the ecclesiastical court for maintenance. Then he would plead successfully that he had no available assets; all his possessions were now *corban*, dedicated to religious uses, and so the judge must dismiss the case. Yet the man who had played this knavish trick on his father and mother might have an untroubled conscience, because he had not violated the Law. And this example did not stand alone; "many such like things ye do," Jesus said, "making the word of God of none effect through your traditions."

As every reader of the Gospels will recollect, the point at which Jesus came most frequently into conflict with the legalistic tradition was that of sabbath-observance. There is no reason to doubt that the sabbath was a festival valued and enjoyed by the Jews, although the pleasure it was meant to bring must often have been greatly lessened by the exceedingly troublesome rules which the Pharisees had devised to guard its sanctity. Many Jewish and some Christian writers have emphasized the fact that for the most minute and grotesque regulations about the sabbath we have to turn to the rabbinic compilation known as the *Mishnah*, and that this was not put together until near the end of the second century A.D. Therefore, it is urged, we are unjustified in quoting these later rules as though they were in force during our Lord's days on earth. Further, it is said that they represent the academic views and themes for disputation of the rabbis rather than regulations which were actually enforced. On the other hand, such a compilation as the *Mishnah* is not the fruit of sudden invention; far more probably its rules had been in existence long before they were codified and set down in a formal treatise. Again, while it seems probable that different schools of rabbinic tradition applied the sabbatical rules with different degrees of strictness, so that what one deemed serious sin was thought unimportant or permissible by the other, the Gospels and the words of our Lord himself show quite plainly that in his time the rules of sabbath-observance were rigid and often absurd. The disciples were supposed to have "worked" on the sabbath, and therefore to have sinned, when they rubbed ears of wheat between their hands. Our Lord was repeatedly attacked for healing on the sabbath, because to heal was to work. Thus a rabbinic decision of a later date held that it was lawful to apply a bandage to a wound on the sabbath, but not to place ointment on the bandage, because the ointment would heal. A woman must not look in the mirror on the sabbath, lest she notice a grey hair and be tempted to pull it out. Water must not be heated; if use is made of any that was heated before the sabbath began (at 6 p.m. on Friday evening), care must be taken lest the steam from it should accidentally cleanse the walls. What might be done with an egg which a depraved hen had been wicked enough to lay on the sabbath? This point seems to have been discussed at length. Rabbis of the school of Hillel said that to eat such an egg was to profane the sabbath, but those of the school of Shammai took the opposite view.

These rules are only a few examples drawn from a great number. It has been urged that they merely represent rabbinic casuistry and were no more than themes for ingenious argument and debate, being never enforced in practice. At least, however, they show the spirit in which sabbath-observance was interpreted, while the Gospel narratives and our Lord's sayings leave us in no doubt that some at least of the rabbis in his time did teach that every devout Jew was bound in conscience to obey such rules. Those concessions which were made resembled the rules themselves in character. Thus a man must not travel farther than "a sabbath day's journey"— 2,000 cubits, about 1,000 yards. But he was permitted to look at some tree on the horizon and to say aloud "I make my sabbath home under the shade of that tree." Then his walk to the tree would not count, and the 2,000 cubits he was allowed would not begin until he had reached it.

v

What, then, are we to suppose was the effect of this legalism, this intricate and artificial system of religion, upon the life and thought of the Palestinian Jew? In theory, as expounded officially by the rabbis, it dominated his whole existence. To quote Schürer; (*The Jewish People in the Time of Jesus Christ*, Div. ii., vol. 2, p. 125):

> Nothing was left to free personality, everything was placed under the bondage of the letter. The Israelite, zealous for the Law, was obliged at every impulse and movement to ask himself, what is commanded? At every step, at the work of his calling, at prayer, at meals, at home and abroad, from early morning till late in the evening, from youth to old age, the dead, the deadening formula followed him. A healthy moral life could not flourish under such a burden, action was nowhere the result of inward motive, all was, on the contrary, weighed and measured. Life was a continual torment to the earnest man, who felt at every moment that he was in danger of transgressing the Law.

Yet a knowledge of human nature will suggest that it is unsafe to generalize in this fashion. No doubt there were many who did feel legalism as a crushing load; our Lord rebuked the rabbis who "bind heavy burdens and grievous to be borne, and lay them on men's shoulders"; he offered rest for the soul of those who were weary and heavy-laden under such burdens. But we may doubt if the average trader or farmer or fisherman, especially in Galilee, shared this feeling to any great extent.

Such people had found long ago that in practice no ordinary man or woman could possibly keep the Law, or get through a day without transgressing one of its technical commands or prohibitions. Yet a knowledge of human nature may make us doubt if for this reason "life was a continual torment" to the average Galilean. More probably he had ceased to trouble very much about it. He would not openly rebel against the Law; he would not violate the sabbath, for instance, in a flagrant fashion, which would have led to his expulsion from the synagogue. But, speaking generally, he would regard legalism, the official religion, as something outside his reach. The complete obedience to a code which it demanded was possible only for exceptional people, like the Pharisees; for others to attempt it was simply not worth while. To attribute this attitude to the Galileans is not merely conjecture. Their disregard of the Law was notorious, and "this multitude which knoweth not the Law are accursed" was the way in which they were described by the official religious leaders at Jerusalem.

But this does not mean that they were irreligious. They were discontented and restless because the official religion, even if all its demands could be exactly fulfilled, was unable to satisfy the hunger of their souls. They listened eagerly when passages from the prophets were read in the synagogue, and contrasted their spiritual teaching with that given by the scribes. In far-off days the prophets had seen the danger that mere compliance with a code and the elaborate sacrificial ritual of the Temple would be regarded as the whole duty of man, and that the inner religion of heart and will would be neglected. Some seven hundred years before our Lord's time Micah had set forth the truth magnificently:

> Wherewith shall I come before the Lord,
> And bow myself before the high God?
> Will the Lord be pleased with thousands of rams,
> Or with ten thousand rivers of oil?
>
> Shall I give my first-born for my transgression,
> The fruit of my body for the sin of my soul?
> He hath showed thee, O man, what is good;
> And what doth the Lord require of thee
> But to do justly,
> And to love mercy,
> And to walk humbly with thy God?

This, the religion taught by the prophets, was the kind of religion which the simple Galilean folk felt that they needed. To be honest and upright, to be kind and forbearing, to live as in God's sight and trying always to do his will—that was an ideal which touched the conscience, one which the plain man could constantly try to attain. How different it was from legalism, with its complicated technical code, its almost innumerable regulations for the sabbath, its insistence that to break any of its requirements was a sin against God! True, the written Law as supplied by the Scriptures was comparatively simple; it might not always be easy to observe, yet at least the Jew could know whether he was obeying it. But in our Lord's time, the "Tradition" of the scribes not merely vastly elaborated, but was held superior to, the written code. What ordinary man could know how rabbinic authority had decided what he must do or abstain from doing in regard to a thousand disputable points? Again, some of the prophets had refused to think of Yahweh as a merely national deity. They were sure that he had a special and unique relationship with Israel, but held that his mercies extended to the Gentiles also, and that ultimately these races would be brought into his kingdom. In short, there were discrepancies and consequent opposition between the legalistic and prophetic schools of thought.

The influence of the prophets was strongest during the troubled period before the Exile and during the Exile itself. The destruction of the Temple meant the end, for the time being, of the elaborate sacrificial system linked with the Law. But legalism began to reassert itself with the return to Jerusalem of some of the exiles and the reconstruction of the Temple, and increasingly it became the dominant force in the religion of Israel. As Dr. R. H. Charles wrote (*Between the Old and New Testaments*, p. 41, &c.):

From Nehemiah's time onward prophecy could not gain a hearing, unless it was acceptable in the eyes of the Law . . . God, according to the official teachers, had spoken his last and final word through the Law, and when the hope is expressed that in the coming age a prophet will arise, he was conceived of only as one whose task was to decide questions of ritual, or priestly succession, or legal interpretation in accordance with the Law . . . From the time of Ezra and Nehemiah the Law not only assumed the functions of the pre-Exilic prophets but also, so far as lay in its power, made the revival of such prophecy an impossibility.

Yet it would be a mistake to assume that the prophetic type of religion had ceased to have any influence in our Lord's days. True, legalism, and legalism alone, had become the official religion of the Palestinian Jews. Yet the prophetical books were read in the synagogue services and spoke their clear message, however astutely the rabbis might expound them to uphold their own views. Again, the apocalyptic literature, begun when prophecy had been silenced and still being produced, contained teaching closely in line with that of the prophets. It is true that the apocalyptic books did not count as Scripture and were not read in the synagogue services, yet their influence was considerable. But the strongest factor of all in reviving the prophetic type of religion was the mission of John the Baptist. After an interval of more than four centuries a mysterious figure, clothed like Elijah, appeared in the desert, and taught as the prophets of old had done. The religion he preached seemed wholly unlike that upheld by the Pharisees. It called for repentance, it awoke conscience, it stirred a sense of sin, it swept away the idea that all must be well in God's sight with those who belonged to his chosen race: "think not to say within yourselves, We have Abraham to our father; for I say unto you that God is able of these stones to raise up children unto Abraham." No, they must bring forth "fruits meet for repentance" and that quickly; the time was short, the axe at the root of the tree, the kingdom of God at hand!

No wonder that multitudes of people with starved souls answered this call, hung on John's words, welcomed his teaching, were baptized by him as a sign of their repentance. So, though without any approval from the accredited religious leaders, the prophetic strain of teaching was revived. When a still more wonderful new teacher, Jesus of Nazareth, began his ministry, the question would be widely asked: "On which side is he? Does he support the official religion and the Law, or is he of the prophetic school, like John?" On the one hand, he spoke on subjects, such as prayer and fasting and sabbath-observance, which were themes permitted to rabbis alone; yet on the other what he said, with its call to repentance and announcement of the kingdom of God, was closely in line with the prophetic message of John. Our Lord was careful to answer this question. He upheld both the Law and the prophetic teaching; he planned to fill both with new significance. "Think not that I am come to destroy the Law or the prophets; I am not come to destroy, but to fulfil." He was no opponent of the Law, but only of the rabbinic legalism, "the traditions of men" which perverted the true meaning and purpose of the Law. He himself would reinterpret and amplify it, but in ways wholly different from those of the rabbis.

VI

The facts, then, we have reviewed in this chapter may help us to answer the questions suggested at its beginning:—what religious foundation did our Lord find on which to build? What were the beliefs of the people among whom he lived? How far did those beliefs help or hinder his work? We have noted that the people were, as a whole, deeply, even uniquely, religious, and that religion was the predominant factor in their education, culture and outlook. We saw that in its early form it had provided a lofty if narrow creed, and that in the course of centuries it had been notably enriched, both by the teaching of the prophets and by such foreign influences as that which developed belief in personal immortality. And we shall not be wrong to conclude that the religious setting in which our Lord found his contemporaries aided his mission in some ways, and thwarted it in others.

As in the political and economic realms, the prevailing religious mood of Palestine at this time was one of expectant and often dissatisfied unrest. Pharisaic legalism was the creed with the greatest weight of official authority behind it. The Pharisees themselves were, for the most part, sincerely contented with it; this, as our Lord saw it, was the supreme tragedy of their attitude. The Sadducees detested the Pharisees, rejected their "Tradition," but upheld the Law, because the Law meant the Temple system, and the Temple system meant for the Sadducees an influence out of proportion to their numbers, and substantial wealth. The common people were treated by the Pharisees with an arrogance and contempt which were often insufferable. They had no liking for the Sadducees, who flourished on those Temple offerings and dues which the people had to pay. And the genuine soul-hunger of the ordinary folk could not be satisfied by legalism.

So far, therefore, the prevalent conditions assisted our Lord's ministry, bringing him at once an immense body of listeners. Despite the anger of the official religious leaders, multitudes gathered to hear him who spoke as never man spoke. And the Master had compassion on them, and taught them, though there were times when, worn out by the strain of this work, he had to try to escape from them. At a later stage he ceased his public teaching in order to concentrate on the training of his disciples, but towards the end, when he was nearing Jerusalem, as Mark relates, "multitudes came together unto him again; and as he was wont, he taught them again." Yet he realized the limitations of this method, this scattering of the seed broadcast; the proportion that fell on good ground was so small! Some listened from mere curiosity, some in the hope of seeing miracles, a large number in the confident belief that he would lead a movement for political and economic reform, and so lighten their financial burdens.

The plan with which our Lord began his ministry in Galilee was, quite evidently, to use the machinery of the national church as the means of distributing his message. Accordingly as he went from place to place it was in the local synagogues that he preached, and, at first, with the full support—indeed, at the invitation of—the Galilean synagogue-authorities. But when the character of his teaching, which they regarded as subversive and mischievous, was reported to the head authorities at Jerusalem, they issued instructions to the local rulers of the synagogues in Galilee that on no account must he be allowed in future to preach in the buildings they controlled. Therefore the plan had to be changed. The multitudes were still friendly, but he could not depend on them for the continuous transmission and propagation of his Gospel. For this he must rely on a few chosen men, whom he would train intensively, so that they might be able to proclaim his message when his own stay in this world was ended. As against, then, the popular welcome which he received, we have to set the fact that the official leaders of the national religion in Palestine opposed our Lord with increasing hatred, and at length succeeded in bringing about his death. So we see him at work among a vast population which, from various motives, was eager to hear him, while at the same time every effort to check his influence, to discredit his doctrine, and presently to kill him, was made for political reasons by a set of leaders who represented officially the national church of Palestine.

CHAPTER FIVE

LEADERS AND CENTRES OF RELIGION

I

THE Jews of Palestine, as has been remarked on an earlier page, were organized as a church rather than as a nation. It follows that among such a people the religious leaders were of high importance. They figure prominently in the Gospel stories, they influenced the daily life in which our Lord moved, and to have some accurate knowledge of them is essential to a right understanding of the Gospels. Yet popular ideas about them are often vague or misinformed. Perhaps many Bible-readers would accept, for example, Dr. Johnson's description—I quote from the first edition of his dictionary:—"The sect of the Pharisees, whose religion consisted almost wholly in ceremonies"; whereas the Pharisees were not a sect, and their religion was by no means such as Dr. Johnson supposed. The scribe is sometimes imagined to have been a man who spent his days in copying out the Scriptures, while the Sadducee is thought of as a kind of agnostic. Unless we have an adequate knowledge of these people and what they believed, we shall miss the point of our Lord's words on page after page of the Gospels.

We may begin with the scribes. In an earlier age they had been, as their name suggests, almost solely copyists and students of the sacred Law—men whose work, as we should say, was done in the study rather than in public. But their functions had become very much wider in the New Testament period. They were now the authorized religious teachers. In our English Bible they appear sometimes as "scribes," sometimes as "lawyers" and sometimes as "doctors of the Law," but each of these terms describes the same men. A teacher was a "rab," and the scribe was addressed as "rabbi," which means literally "my teacher," although the force of the suffix had disappeared, like the force of the prefix in "monsieur" and "madame." Probably it was only as a form of address, a sign of honour, that "rabbi" was used in the Gospel period; not until a later time did it become a generic description. Yet to use it in this way is convenient; if we term these men "rabbis" instead of "scribes" we avoid the misunderstanding which the latter name suggests—and it was at no long time after our Lord's age that they were commonly described, and not merely addressed, as rabbis.

They were, then, the authorized teachers of religion, the expounders of that Tradition which they ranked as more important than the Law itself, and the judges in the local ecclesiastical courts. Often a devout Jew would be genuinely perplexed to know what he might or might not do according to the Law, as interpreted and amplified by the Tradition. Only a rabbi could give him the decision he needed. Apart, too, from answering genuine questions, the rabbis loved to discuss imaginary cases. If this or the other situation arose, what did the Tradition permit? For instance, if your house caught fire on the sabbath, were you permitted to rescue your clothing? Only what was necessary, said the official ruling. You might put on a dress, take it to a place of safety, return and put on another dress, rescue that, and so on. The rabbis alone could give an authoritative judgment on the innumerable problems arising from sabbath-observance. They only could give direction about marriage and divorce, fasting, prayer and other religious duties—every judgment being based upon a careful collation of the Law itself with the interpretations given it by eminent rabbis of the past. This process was complicated by the fact that often there had been considerable divergence of opinion among the rabbis themselves. The school of thought founded by Shammai, for instance, was stricter in its interpretation of the Law and more severe in the penalties exacted for its breach than was the rival school of Hillel. The rabbis who followed the Hillel tradition held that a badly-cooked dinner justified a man in divorcing his wife, while the Shammai school taught that adultery alone justified divorce. When the Pharisees asked our Lord: "Is it lawful for a man to put away his wife for every cause?" the real point of their question was; "Are you a teacher of the Shammai or of the Hillel school of thought?"

The rabbis loved such discussion for its own sake. When debating the Law they would cite the Scriptures with minute attention to ingenious verbal quibbles. St. Paul in his Christian days never wholly lost his fondness for the arguments of this type, which he had learned as the pupil of Gamaliel, the famous Hillel's famous grandson. In Galatians iii. 16: "He saith not, And to seeds, as of many; but as of one, And to thy seed, which is Christ," we have a typical example of the rabbinical method. As Professor G. S. Duncan remarks in his commentary on the passage, "Paul must have known that neither in Hebrew nor in Greek did the plural of the word in question indicate a difference of meaning from the singular such as he here suggests." Yet, if worthless in itself, it was an argument of the kind in which any Jewish readers of his letter would delight.

II

The more famous rabbis had schools of their own in which they received their pupils. Sometimes, especially at the great festivals, they taught publicly, in the courts of the Temple, holding catechetical classes, in which learners were encouraged to propound problems of conduct and to ask questions. It was such a class which our Lord attended in his boyhood. Many of these scribes or rabbis travelled from place to place, accompanied by disciples. Often when such a rabbi reached a town or village he would be asked, as a matter of courtesy—and the more readily were he well known—to preach in the synagogue on the next sabbath. So it was that our Lord was invited during the earlier days of his ministry in Galilee. Anyone who was asked, a layman, as we should say, might give moral teaching in a synagogue, but the privilege of expounding the Law and Tradition was strictly confined to the rabbis. At a time later than that of the Gospels they were appointed to this work by a form of ordination. Though this rite was not yet in use in the New Testament period, there seems no reason to doubt Edersheim's statement that "it is at least certain that, at the time of our Lord, no one would have ventured authoritatively to teach without proper rabbinic authorization." Jesus always taught "as one having authority" on subjects limited to scribes, and not until the last days in Jerusalem had he to meet the challenge, "by what authority?"

Besides the famous rabbis who were the greatly-honoured heads of their profession, there were very many others, some in Judaea, a large number in Galilee, who lived in the towns and villages, taught in the synagogues and in the schools attached to them, and presided over the local ecclesiastical courts. St. Luke mentions (v. 17) that on one day when our Lord was teaching there were "doctors of the Law sitting by, which were come out of every village of Galilee and Judaea and Jerusalem." "Every" is a word of which this evangelist often makes picturesque use and need not be taken literally, yet this verse at least shows that the number of rabbis was very considerable, and that they were to be found in villages as well as in towns. In this as in many other passages the scribes are linked with the Pharisees. It seems certain that a large majority of them were members of that body. A few were Sadducees, but these would seldom be found in Galilee.

III

The Pharisees were a kind of guild or society, containing both rabbis and a far greater proportion of layfolk. Neither Pharisees nor Sadducees should be described as a "sect." That term properly denotes people who have "cut themselves off" from the national church and created an organization of their own. The only important "sect" in Palestine during the Gospel period was that of the Essenes, and of them there is no direct mention, though there are allusions to their ascetic doctrine. Both Pharisees and Sadducees, though there was bitter antagonism between them, claimed to be ardent supporters of the Law, the Sadducees as its guardian against unauthorized additions, the Pharisees as interpreting and developing it to meet every need of life.

The historian Josephus estimated the numbers of the Pharisaic guild at six thousand, and, untrustworthy as his figures often are, this may be approximately correct. The Pharisees were always eager to gain new members; they would "move heaven and earth to make one proselyte," our Lord said. In theory, there was a form of election for admission into the fraternity, but the wife and children of a Pharisee became members automatically; St. Paul, for instance, was one as being the son of a Pharisee. The chief aim of the fraternity in its early days had been to preserve the Jews, God's chosen people, from foreign influence in general and Graeco-Roman influence in particular. While adhering to this ideal their primary object in the New Testament account had come to be the exact observance of the Law as set forth in rabbinic Tradition. This alone, they claimed, was the true creed of Judaism. They alone were faithful to it, and therefore they alone were acceptable in God' sight. They despised the Jews outside their ranks, terming them "the people of the land," the common herd.

Most of the rabbis, as has been noted, were members of this fraternity, but the average Pharisee whom we might have met in Capernaum or Nazareth in our Lord's time would be a well-to-do middle-class layman. It would be easy to recognize him. His "phylacteries"—little leather cases containing words of the Law, strapped across the forehead and left arm—were "broader" than those of other men, and the fringe attached to his garment was "enlarged." With ostentatious piety he would halt in the road, preferably at a street corner, to recite his devotions, thanking God he was not as other men. With some of the Pharisees religion was a mere pretence; except when they were in the public eye, they carefully avoided the irksome duties, the punctilious observance of the code, which formed the burden they sought to impose on others. But it is a great mistake to imagine that the average Pharisee was insincere. On the contrary, with all his heart he believed that his view of himself and "the common people" was right, that his arrogance was justified, that the one supreme duty demanded by God was exact fulfilment of the rabbinical code, and that with this the claims of personal religion began and ended. It was, indeed, the sincerity with which he held this creed that made his plight so desperate. The vehemence with which our Lord denounced the Pharisees was due to the fact that no mere persuasion could hope to break through that fatal self-satisfaction in which they had enveloped themselves. The Pharisee of the parable was a man of strict life and, according to his lights, of austere piety. The publican was stained by gross sin. But for the publican, now that he was penitent, gradual progress towards real holiness was possible; the path lay clear before him. For the Pharisee, on the contrary, there could be no progress; his fundamentally wrong beliefs, his atrophied conscience, and, above all, his utter self-complacency interposed a barrier beyond which he could not pass.

Yet, except for those few whose religion was a mere pretence, the life of the Pharisee must have been far from easy. Unremitting effort and severe self-discipline were necessary to comply, as daily he attempted to do, with all the requirements of the legalistic code. We need not wonder that other people, wounded though they may have been by his unconcealed contempt for them, yet eyed the Pharisee as he passed along the street with an admiring gaze. Here, most of them supposed, was the personification of religion as it should be. Here was one who had succeeded in reaching a standard which seemed utterly beyond their own reach. We must remember, too, that our Lord had friends among the Pharisees, and that such men as Nicodemus certainly would not have been included in his condemnation. Yet the terribly stern character of that utterance does show that, high as might be the characters of individual Pharisees, the fraternity of Pharisaism as a whole was deeply tainted with formalism, with a most unjustified arrogance, with perverted standards that were fatal to the development of religion as interpreted by Christ.

IV

In our Lord's time we should have met Pharisees in every part of Palestine, and the Gospels show that they were numerous in Galilee. But we should seldom have found Sadducees except in Jerusalem and its neighbourhood. The Sadducees, like the Pharisees, could trace their existence back to Old Testament times, and from the beginning there had been keen antagonism between the two bodies. But the Sadducean organization was constituted very differently from the other. Membership in it was far from being thrown open; it was in fact virtually limited to the chief priests and their families, and these, in a society pre-eminently religious, formed the aristocracy of Palestine. Yet, to a great extent, the religion of these people was not much more than normal, and it was for the power and wealth which their high office brought them rather than for its sanctity that they valued it. The Sadducees were far more worldly than the Pharisees, and their chief interests were political rather than religious. In early days they had favoured that introduction of Greek culture into Judaism which seemed sheer sacrilege to the Pharisees. Their religious

creed also was different. We have seen that the Pharisee upheld
the "Tradition," the interpretations and developments of the
rabbis, as even more important than the original Law; the
Sadducee maintained that the Law in its original form alone
had divine authority, and dismissed rabbinic Tradition as
worthless. From this conviction came their disbelief in a
resurrection and future life. With all their worldliness, it
would be unfair to term them materialists or agnostics. But to
every doctrine propounded for their acceptance they applied
one test: "Is there authority for this in the Law of Moses?"
They could discover nothing about resurrection and a future
life in the Law of Moses, therefore the doctrine of resurrection
and a future life must be rejected as false.

There is no trustworthy evidence for computing the
number of the Sadducees, but probably their total did not
amount to more than a few hundreds, while there were several
thousand Pharisees. What is certain is that they were a rela-
tively small body of wealthy aristocrats, in which the chief
priests of Jerusalem and their relatives were prominent.
Among their chief aims, naturally enough, was the maintenance of the Temple system, because from this source, with its
numerous taxes and duties levied in the name of religion, their
large incomes were derived. In an earlier chapter it was
pointed out that the dual taxation—the civil taxes payable to
Rome, the religious taxes payable to the Temple authorities—
had become an almost intolerable burden to the people of
Palestine, and therefore it is not surprising that the Sadducees
were regarded with little favour by the populace. "They only
gain the rich; the people are not on their side," wrote Josephus,
the Jewish historian, of the Sadducees. Their wealth and
official position had given them great influence, but this was
diminished, especially outside Jerusalem, as the power of their
rivals the Pharisees increased. Even in Jerusalem by our Lord's
time some of the Pharisaic scribes had obtained places in the
"Great Sanhedrin," the supreme court of the Jews, which at
an earlier stage had been controlled entirely by the Sadducean
priests.

The immense importance of this Great Sanhedrin needs to
be understood when we read the Gospels and Acts. It dominated the lives of the people. It was a court which had full
ecclesiastical, civil, and criminal jurisdiction. It was the

supreme religious authority; in theory, even the interpretations of the Law given by the most learned rabbis were supposed to have behind them the authority of the Great Sanhedrin in order to be valid. All important civil cases were brought before it, and in criminal cases it had plenary powers, except that when it had pronounced sentence of death this had to be ratified by the Roman procurator before it could be carried out. It consisted of seventy-one members, appointed with solemn ceremonial, and to be a member of the Great Sanhedrin was to be a person of eminence, a leading authority on the divine Law. The high priest seems, *ex officio*, to have been president of the court, and in the Gospel period the majority of members were drawn from the Sadducean priestly aristocracy, although, as has been mentioned, a number of Pharisaic rabbis were also included. All cases of importance were referred to it, as the final court of appeal, by the local courts scattered over the country, and from the Great Sanhedrin official orders would be sent to the rulers of the local synagogues.

A word should be added to guard against possible misunderstanding. While it is true to say that the Great Sanhedrin dealt not only with ecclesiastical but civil and criminal cases, we must remember that the modern distinction between them hardly existed. There were not three codes utilized by the Sanhedrin according to the character of the case before it at the moment. One Law, the Law of Moses, controlled every department of life. In other words, every matter was judged by a single code, the code of religion. Sabbath-breaking was not distinctively an ecclesiastical offence but a crime; theft was a crime, not against society but against the Law of Moses. Deeds of cruelty might be adjudged as less serious offences than some technical infringement of the Law. Thus in his *Jesus of Nazareth* Dr. Klausner, a professing Jew, writes:

> To the orthodox Pharisee (and to the modern orthodox Jew) the violation of the Sabbath and the oppression of the hireling were alike crimes deserving of death, and to the average Jew of all times the former seems the worse crime.

Such a statement may be left to speak for itself.

In addition to this supreme court and religious authority in Jerusalem, every town and most of the larger villages in Palestine had their local Sanhedrins, the members of which were often nominated by the Great Sanhedrin and were also usually the rulers of the local synagogues. They had more direct influence on the lives of ordinary people than the authorities in Jerusalem. They could enforce strict discipline on the lives of the town or village community. Their rule was like that of the kirk elders in a Scottish village of the early nineteenth century. Anyone who affronted them by seemingly lax behaviour, as by disregard of the sabbath Law, would have to appear in their court. If condemned, he would be disgraced and made to do penance; for a serious offence he might suffer a public scourging, and among the synagogue officials was one specially entrusted with the infliction of corporal punishment. If an offender were formally expelled from the synagogue, in effect he was ostracized, and the sentence probably meant his financial as well as social ruin. In the story of the healing of a blind man (John ix) his parents "feared the Jews" and were afraid to attribute the healing to our Lord, "for the Jews had agreed already that if any man should confess him to be Christ, he should be put out of the synagogue." There is no reason to suppose that in normal circumstances the rulers of the synagogue who presided over the local Sanhedrin used their powers tyrannically. But the mere fact that they had these immense powers and kept a watchful eye on the inhabitants of their town or village made people careful not to offend them, and the influence of the local courts and synagogues is a factor not to be ignored when we picture the Gospel background. In particular, it emphasizes one of the perils which those who dared to own their belief in Christ had to face; "they shall put you out of the synagogues," he had warned his disciples, and we need to realize what this involved.

His local synagogue, in short, counted for far more with the average Jew than did the Temple, much as his parish church means more to the average Christian than does the cathedral of his diocese. He had been taught in its school, each sabbath day he attended its service, and its rulers would bring him into court for any religious laxity or civil wrongdoing. Yet it need hardly be said that every pious Jew regarded the Temple with profound veneration; it was the sign, and more than the sign, of Yahweh's presence among his chosen people; God himself drew near, it was believed, when once a year, on the Day of

Atonement, the high priest unaccompanied was allowed to enter the inmost shrine, the Holy of Holies. Apart also from its religious significance, the Temple was a great unifying force for the Jews. Three times in the year, at the Feast of Passover, Pentecost, and Tabernacles, every Jew was supposed to make his pilgrimage to Jerusalem and to join in the Temple worship. Not all did this; the larger part of the nation were not of "the Dispersion," with homes outside Palestine, and those who had to make a sea voyage to Palestine were often content to do this once a year. The Feast of Weeks attracted more of them than Pentecost, because it came later in the year, when the risk of a stormy passage was less.

At each of the three Feasts, however, Jerusalem and its neighbourhood were thronged to overflowing; the number of pilgrims was far larger than the city itself could accommodate. They would spend the night in neighbouring villages or bivouac in fields and orchards, and come into the city and the Temple precincts during the daytime. Such occasions meant the reunion of long-separated friends; they meant also that national feeling rose to its highest. Then most of all rumours of some Messiah, some leader against Rome, became current, and hopes of deliverance from foreign power and foreign taxation were keen. When he came, it was believed, the divinely-sent leader would announce himself in the Temple, and what occasion could be so suitable as a time when one of the great Feasts had brought the people together from every part of Palestine and from many distant lands?

The Temple worship still centred on that elaborate system of sacrifices which contributed to the wealth of the Sadducean priesthood. Sacrifices were offered at the daily morning and evening services, accompanied by blowing of trumpets, clanging of cymbals and chanting of psalms. No doubt forms of prayer and thanksgiving were also used in the Temple.

Synagogues seem first to have been devised by Jews of "the Dispersion," separated by great distances from the Temple, and afterwards to have been introduced into Palestine. In them there was no offering of sacrifices, and their services were far less elaborate than those of the Temple. In modern terms, we should say that they consisted of the reading of Lessons (from the Law and the prophetical books), of set prayers, and of sermons, which, like our Lord's in the synagogue of Nazareth, were usually expositions of a passage that had just been read as a Lesson. There is reason to suppose that the doctrine preached in many of the local synagogues, especially in Galilee, was far less legalistic and far more liberal than that delivered in the Temple. Even in Jerusalem, however, there was, as already has been mentioned, considerable variety of ecclesiastical opinions, with unending wrangles between Pharisee and Sadducee, and disputes between those rabbis who claimed Hillel and those who claimed Shammai as their master.

It is therefore not surprising that the mood of the people among whom our Lord lived was, in regard to religion as well as the economic and political situation, one of disquiet and unrest. The growing unpopularity of the Sadducean priesthood tended to discredit the Temple system. The Pharisees were revered, yet the legalistic code which they upheld seemed impracticable to the average man, and many who had tried to conform with it found that a religion of this external kind could not satisfy their conscience or supply their spiritual needs. The prophetic teaching of the Baptist had deeply moved those who had listened to it, but John was dead. This new teacher, who seemed so curiously to combine the work of a rabbi with doctrines carrying yet further those taught by the Baptist, undoubtedly swayed multitudes and spoke as no other had done. Yet the official leaders of religion denounced him as a blasphemer and had forbidden him to be heard in the synagogues. Every kind of opinion about him could be heard, with rumours as confident as they were contradictory.

Such seem to have been some of the encouragements and difficulties which faced our Lord, such were the religious hopes, fears, prejudices, bewilderments of the Palestinian Jews, when Jesus moved among them with matchless resolve and serenity to proclaim the kingdom of God.

CHAPTER SIX

HOME LIFE

I

To understand the Gospels we need to learn what we can about the home life of the people whom our Lord addressed, for this deeply coloured his teaching. He did not bewilder those simple folk by using the abstract language of philosophy; his illustrations were drawn from their daily routine and from things abundantly familiar to them. Some of the parables, for instance, help us to realize the ordinary life in a house of the humbler class. Every Bible-reader can recall such details—the patching of an old garment, the woman hunting feverishly for her lost coin, the house of such a size that one lamp set on a stand is sufficient to light the whole of it; the householder and his children in the same bed, and the room so small that from his bed the man can carry on a conversation with a neighbour in the street. Or we see the outside stairway to the flat roofs— once serving a whole row of the lesser houses, because their roofs adjoin; often there is an "upper chamber" on the roof, which guests can enter or leave, using the outside stairway, without disturbing the household. During the heat the inhabitants spend much time on the roof, and it is the place of general talk, where what earlier have been confidences are "proclaimed on the housetop."

It is easy, too, to picture the Capernaum in which Christ dwelt. The winding, narrow, roughly-cobbled streets, with the roofs almost meeting at the centre; the noise and gesticulation of the bazaar; beasts of burden tethered; pariah dogs licking the beggar's sores; horrible stenches; the fish-market and fish-curing factory—hence the many allusions to the use of salt—a din of high-pitched voices speaking many languages; a Pharisee posturing at a street corner; devout folk entering the synagogue which a broad-minded Gentile soldier had paid for—these are some details of the scene. When we try to visualize the Gospel background we are sometimes apt to forget that it is oriental, and to endow it in our imagination with the ways and habits of our own race, and even of our own times.

Of course the atmosphere of Capernaum, an important trading centre with a mixed population of perhaps from fifteen to twenty thousand, would be very different from that of Nazareth, our Lord's earlier home. Nazareth was large enough to count as a town rather than a village, yet it was the kind of place where everyone knew everyone else, where everyone's affairs were public property, and all the inhabitants met each sabbath in the place of worship. "Is not this the carpenter?" they exclaimed, when Jesus came back to them as a rabbi; "is not this the son of Mary, and brother of James, and Joses, and Judas, and Simon? And are not his sisters here with us?" The synagogue gave something of a family feeling to the Jews of a place like Nazareth.

Not only were the Palestine Jews orientals, but in regard to general culture they were a backward oriental race. On the other hand, they had a higher conception of family life than any of their contemporaries; far higher, for example, than that which could be found in ancient Greece or Rome. Indeed, a high reverence for home life has always been characteristic of the Jews. Here, when religious, political and class hatreds were painfully evident, our Lord could find a type of unvarying affection which would serve to give men some idea of the love of God. And that type was the love of a father for his children. The people to whom he spoke had many faults, yet he could be sure that not one of them who was a father would fail, if he could help it, to supply his son's needs. We may observe, too, how specially compassionate our Lord shows himself to widows; how he raised the widow's son, how he attacks the scribes who "devour widows' houses," and we remember that his own mother was almost certainly a widow when the words were spoken. We know how he loved little children, and watched them playing at weddings and funerals, imitating the music of the pipes, the wails of professional mourners. Was his own favourite game in the days of child-hood that of playing at being a rabbi, while other children sat round him as pupils? It seems possible enough, if we recall the visit to Jerusalem when he was twelve, and what he would be likely to do after his return to the other children of Nazareth.

Why was this an episode which Mary kept in her heart with special care, and why, when St. Luke had heard it from her, did he think it so significant that, for this once, he must lift the veil which otherwise was kept drawn between the time of the birth and the beginning of the public ministry? Because, we may believe, it showed that Jesus had resolved, as children will, what he would be when he was grown up. Already, in a way that amazed his hearers, he was keenly interested in religious teaching; it was a religious teacher, a scribe, a rabbi, that he meant to become. Perhaps Mary and Joseph smiled, for they thought that always he would have to follow Joseph's trade. Yet Mary, as mothers love to do, kept his words in her heart and remembered that childish ambition.

II

It was from his mother and Joseph that Jesus would be given his earliest religious teaching; custom prescribed that it should begin almost as soon as a child could speak. Among his earliest memories would be of those family prayers, of lighted candles and little ceremonies which marked special days in every Jewish home, and of the many things which, permissible through the rest of the week, were forbidden him on the sabbath. When a child was five or six, he began to attend the local school, which usually was held in, or was attached to, the synagogue. A course of instruction recommended by rabbinic authorities was that the pupil should learn the Scriptures, especially the Law, up to the age of ten, after which for the next five years he should be instructed in the Tradition. At the age of fifteen, pupils who had shown special aptitude might be sent—as was St. Paul—to study under some famous rabbi at Jerusalem. Rabbinical schools for "advanced" pupils were established also in other parts of Palestine, but they seem to have belonged to a period later than that when our Lord was being educated.

When, however, we use the word "education," we need to remember how strictly limited its scope was. Beyond learning how to read and write, the average Palestinian Jew had no intellectual training except in this one subject, the religion of the Law, but in this his training was full and continuous. He did not cease to be taught by his parents when he began to attend the synagogue school. When he left school, it was only to take his place in what we might term the "adult class" of the synagogue. For these were fully as much places of instruction as of worship. Sometimes a visiting rabbi would come and take his place on the raised platform, while the people gathered round and sat on low benches "at his feet," as St. Paul sat at the feet of Gamaliel. The chief method employed by the rabbis was to make their pupils learn by heart passages of Scripture, extracts from the "Tradition" and rules of conduct which seemed of special importance. To aid this process, they would arrange the sentences symmetrically, or clothe them in an epigrammatic form, so that they could the more easily be memorized. Then the teacher would make his class repeat the words after him many times, until they were well known. It will be realized that in days when writing was something of an elaborate business the average memory was far better developed and more retentive than it is in our own age. Again, the rabbis often embodied in parables the lessons they wished to enforce. Many of these stories have survived in rabbinic writings; speaking generally, they are longer, more involved, and without the charm and human interest of those which came from Christ. Yet there is no reason to doubt that our Lord, teaching as a rabbi, used in the main the rabbinic methods. The careful structure of the Lord's Prayer, for instance, with its three petitions for human needs following three for God's glory, is the type of instruction that would be repeated with the disciples until it was fixed in their memories. The Matthaean Gospel gives us many examples of teaching grouped and arranged in lesson-form. And behind the written Gospels was the oral tradition, the memorized accounts of what Jesus had taught.

In addition to the mental education, so systematic and thorough-going in regard to religion, as the national church interpreted it, and so lamentably deficient in every other branch of culture, a Jewish custom seems to have required every boy to be instructed in some trade or handicraft, in order that he might be able to earn a livelihood when he grew up. Apparently this excellent rule applied to all male children, without regard to the financial position of their parents. Wisely enough, it was enforced as a precaution. No one could anticipate what change of fortune might overtake the rich man's son; what the rule could ensure was that, should the need arise, his early training would have made him competent to earn his living. St. Paul's father, for example, must have been at least fairly well-to-do, but the young Paul was taught the craft of weaving tent-cloth, and, as his letters show, in later years he met his personal expenses by this means.

Very often a boy learnt the trade or craft or other business which was practised by his father. Our Lord, as we know, followed that of Joseph. There is much to be said for the view that we should translate *tektôn* by "builder" rather than "carpenter"; the builder at this period being a worker in stone and clay as well as wood. St. Paul, it will be remembered, compares his work in founding churches with that of an *architektôn*, a "master-builder"—whence our word "architect"; and in our own country the early master-builders were in fact the architects, the designers, of the buildings they made. In Palestine the chief business of the worker in wood and stone would be that of house construction; in Jerusalem an immense number must have been employed in the rebuilding of the Temple, which, begun on a vast scale by Herod the Great in 19 B.C., was not completed until A.D. 63—only seven years before the destruction by Roman armies which "left not one stone upon another." But no doubt our Lord was employed upon local work in the neighbourhood of Nazareth. A remarkable saying is attributed to him by a papyrus: "Raise the stone, and there thou shalt find me; cleave the wood, and there am I." If the saying is authentic—a point incapable of proof or disproof—it acquires new force if it were spoken as he contemplated some building on which he had been employed as a worker in stone and wood. And were he builder, not carpenter only, there seems added significance in "on this rock I, the builder, will build my church." We recollect, too, the stories he told about the man who begins to build a tower without having troubled to secure an estimate, about the men whose houses were based on rock and sand. Was it as to an expert that the group of fishermen turned for an opinion about the masonry of the Temple? When, once more, he adapts from

Isaiah a parable about a man planting a vineyard, the details of
the work he mentions are such as might have come within his
own experience—not the agricultural work, but the putting up
of a palisade, and digging a pit for the wine-press, and building
a watch-tower.

III

One respect in which the Palestinian Jews rose above the
ordinary level of Eastern races in the first century was their
high standard of moral purity and their treatment of women.
Indeed, their tendency, often repeated in later ages, was
towards condemning sexual offences with disproportionate
severity. Few things which our Lord did more genuinely
shocked the religious leaders of his day than his readiness to
extend compassion and forgiveness to a woman "who was a
sinner." We recall the beautiful picture which St. Luke gives
us. How could a common street-walker come to own a very
costly vessel of perfume ? It can only have been given her as
part of her hire by one of her lovers, and it was with a fine and
dramatic gesture of renunciation that she poured it over the
Master's feet.

We should notice the great importance attached to betrothal
in Jewish domestic life. Betrothal was a formal and solemn
ceremony, as binding as marriage itself. A man could only
cancel it by divorce, and a woman who was unfaithful after
betrothal was legally accounted an adulteress, and liable, under
the strict letter of the Law, to the penalty of death. To remember this is to find an added poignancy in the story of
Joseph and Mary, his betrothed, as related in the Matthaean
Gospel. The solemn ritual of betrothal seems to have made any
religious ceremonial of the marriage itself unnecessary, but it
was celebrated by a procession of the bride to the bridegroom's
house and by a marriage feast, given in the house of the bridegroom. The scene at Cana depicts for us the marriage feast in a
household of modest means, while our Lord's parable of the
marriage feast made by the king for his son illustrates the
lavish hospitality which accompanied the event among the
rich. One incident of it seems to have been the gift of a new
robe to each of the guests as he entered the house, and in the

story it was the churlish refusal of a guest to accept the gift
which brought upon him the king's anger. Even among the
peasant-folk of Galilee a wedding was the occasion of great
rejoicing and merriment, and, if the means of the bridegroom
or his parents permitted, the festivities would be prolonged
through several days.

The evidence of secular historians shows that polygamy was
still permitted to the Jews in New Testament times. In
practice, however, it seems to have been confined to a few
wealthy and worldly people. It had become repugnant to both
religious and family instincts, while the economic situation in
Palestine was also a more prosaic but effective deterrent.
Divorce, as has been mentioned on an earlier page, was a
subject on which controversy between the two chief schools of
rabbinic thought was specially acute. The followers of Hillel
were ready to sanction divorce on almost any ground; those of
Shammai held that adultery alone justified divorce. (It must be
noted that "adultery" was a term applied to a wife's unfaithful-
ness only; no remedy was provided for a wife whose husband
was unfaithful.) On most points our Lord's doctrine was far
more akin to the liberalism of Hillel than to the rigorism of
Shammai, but over this question of divorce he took the
stricter view. Probably we should be misled if this rabbinic
dispute and the fact that it was one of their favourite themes of
debate caused us to believe that divorce, or an attempt at
divorce, was anything like a normal incident of Jewish life.
The rabbis loved discussion for discussion's sake; their talk
was ever of what was and what was not permissible according
to rival interpretations of the Law; whether the actual situation about which they argued occurred often, or seldom or
never in real life concerned them far less than that they had
found a good theme for argument and counter-argument.
Divorces, of course, there were, and some of them on ludi-
crously trivial grounds; even the fact that the husband has seen
a woman whom he thinks more beautiful than his wife is held
by one rabbinic authority to provide sufficient reason for a
divorce. But, taken as a whole, the domestic life of the people
among whom our Lord worked seems to have been happy and
tranquil. If the womenfolk, according to modern ideas, were
not given their due place, at least they had far more liberty and

greater honour than were allowed to the women of other oriental nations at this period. If Pharisaic legalism had done much to debase the character of the early Law, it had not changed that essential family life, that deep affection between parents and children, which, based on religion, had become from primitive times, and remains to this day, one of the noblest traditions of the Jewish race.

It was, we may believe, in the happiness of family life, in the observance of little feast-days with their cheerful ritual, in the mirth and goodwill of an occasional marriage-supper, that many of our Lord's Galilean neighbours found some solace for the grievous public and private anxieties of the time. These continued to increase, and the ferment was destined to grow until ultimately it brought about open rebellion and complete ruin. The final stage would not be reached until forty years after the Ascension, yet our Lord foresaw plainly what the end would be. Each year the political and economic outlook darkened, while vague religious discontent increased. In spite of the reverence for the sacred city and the traditions of the Temple, in spite of the self-satisfaction of the Pharisees and the rigid conservatism of the Sadducees, men's consciences were dissatisfied by legalism, the official creed of the day. They waited eagerly for a national leader; they were as sheep without a shepherd. Meanwhile, they must carry on their daily tasks, even while deeply anxious about their welfare and even their food for the morrow. Rumours, excited talk, whispers of plots, reports of what this strange new rabbi had taught and done, ardent wishes, gloomy forebodings—these formed the atmosphere in which men talked as they gathered in a market-place or the streets of Jerusalem; this was the setting in which Jesus must strive to preach his Gospel and to found a kingdom not of this world.

CHAPTER SEVEN

PUBLIC OPINION AND OUR LORD

1

THE previous chapters have attempted to sketch in outline the political-economic, the religious and the social background of the Gospels, because to realize the setting in which our Lord moved helps us to understand and to interpret rightly those records of his work which the evangelists have given us. But this study suggests a question which should be answered before we end, because the answer is a further help to reading the Gospels intelligently. If these were the ways and views of the people of Palestine as our Lord found them, how on their part did the people of Palestine view him? And, in particular, what were the source and causes of that bitter hatred which ultimately brought about his Crucifixion? It is the more worth while to examine that point because misunderstandings about it are common.

If we had been able to wander through Palestine and to ask those who had seen and heard Jesus of Nazareth what they thought of him, obviously we should have had a great variety of replies. There were men and women who dared to hope that he would prove to be the promised Messiah. Many would extol him as a most amazing teacher, who moved them and touched their consciences as no other had done. Many would have been impressed chiefly by the marvellous works of healing they had witnessed. Many would own themselves frankly perplexed; on the one hand, they could not deny the mysterious power of his words and deeds; on the other, his doctrine seemed dangerously unorthodox, and the heads of the national church denounced it. Some would pity him as a madman, some would urge that he ought at once to be imprisoned, if not put to death, on the ground that he was a blasphemer, who accomplished his miracles through the agency of evil spirits. Speaking generally, his ardent supporters would be found, and found in very considerable numbers, among the peasant-folk of Galilee, and his most bitter enemies among the Sadducean priests at Jerusalem.

Though there would have been a wide diversity of opinion about his character, it is improbable that there would have been any about the calling he followed. By friends and foes alike he was regarded as a teacher of religion, a scribe, one to be addressed as "rabbi"—"which is to say, teacher" adds the Fourth Gospel. The use of the word "master" in our English version of the Gospels is apt to mislead, because it denotes the relationship of an employer with his servants as well as that of a teacher with his pupils. The marginal notes in the Revised Version, however, are careful to make it clear that the latter is the meaning of "master" in the Gospels. We should notice how our Lord is addressed as "teacher" by people of all kinds and at all moments—for example, by the disciples in extreme distress ("Teacher, carest thou not that we perish?"), by the Pharisees ("Teacher, we know that thou teachest rightly"), by Mary Magdalene in that moment of supreme emotion when she recognizes the risen Lord, even by Iscariot, when he says, "Hail, Teacher," and gives his traitor's kiss.

In fact, there seems little reason to doubt that our Lord resolved to live and work as a rabbi until the right moment had come for him to announce himself as the divine Messiah. To quote Dr. Klausner's words (*Jesus of Nazareth*, p. 254) about the early ministry—and they are the words, it should be noted, of a professing Jew writing for his co-religionists:

> Jesus did not proclaim himself or allow himself to be proclaimed as Messiah till much later. Even to his disciples he did not at first divulge the fact, and when they had realized it for themselves he did not deny it, yet desired them not to make the matter known. He resisted the temptation, and only disclosed himself as a rabbi and simple Galilean preacher, as nothing more than one of the Pharisees or scribes.

Speaking of our Lord's visit to Nazareth, Dr. Swete wrote (*Commentary on Mark*, vi. 1): "It was not a private visit to his family; he came as a rabbi, surrounded by his scholars."

If we ask why our Lord chose to carry on his work in the guise of a rabbi or scribe, the answer is not difficult to surmise. We have noted the seeming conflict of thought between the

Law and the prophets. The Baptist had renewed the teaching of prophecy as against the Law; "all men counted John a prophet." Would Jesus, who began by reiterating John's message, take the same course? Would he uphold prophecy at the expense of the Law, or support the Law and discredit prophecy? He insisted that he would support both. There were times when the prophetic strain predominated in his teaching. "This is Jesus, the prophet of Galilee," was a description of him given by people who, perhaps a few hours earlier, had listened to his lament over Jerusalem and his prediction of its doom.

Yet he was not a prophet hostile to the Law. Nothing of the Law, he insisted, should pass away. Not to the Law, but to misapplications and perversions of the Law, was he opposed. His mission was to attack mere legalism while upholding and fulfilling the Law. Yet the multitudes, under the sway of Pharisaic Judaism, regarded the two as one; to honour the Law, they imagined, you must comply with every rule of the legalistic code. How then, since he was bound to attack legalism, could our Lord best help people to realize that he was not attacking the Law? By coming before them as one of the Law's authorized interpreters and upholders—in other words, as a rabbi or scribe.

In fact, it seems clear that this course was essential if he were to carry out his aim of speaking about the Law, of discussing the duties it prescribed, and of freeing them from the accretions of legalism. Anyone might speak on religion in general, or debate questions of morals or ethics. But to expound in public matters covered by the Law, to teach, as Jesus wished to do, about sabbath-observance, fasting, marriage, prayer, and the Traditions—"it was said by them of old time"—was a right strictly limited to the scribes. Had anyone usurped the scribe's prerogative, the people would not have listened, and he would promptly have been interrupted and arrested. Yet our Lord, because he was accepted as a scribe, did speak, at length and without interruption, on these special themes.

Naturally enough, the crowds were "increasingly amazed" as they listened to the doctrine of this supposed scribe. "What is this?" they exclaimed. "A new teaching!" Almost all the commentators seem to have missed the real point of the sentence (Matt. vii. 29; Mark i. 22): "the people were astonished at his doctrine, for he taught them as one having authority, and not as the scribes." With hardly an exception, they take this to mean that our Lord's teaching was independent, whereas the scribes based theirs on precedent. This is true enough, but it does not seem to be the point which the evangelists here wished to make. They would not have implied that the scribes taught "as not having authority," because authority to teach and interpret the Law was precisely what they, and no others, did possess. Our Lord assumed this authority, so that all his hearers accepted him as an authorized scribe. He sat down to teach, as the scribes did; like the scribes, he used parables; he handled themes which only a scribe might touch. The word to be noticed is the little conjunction *kai*, which, like our own "and," has several shades of meaning. Dr. A. T. Robertson (*Grammar of the Greek New Testament*, p. 1182) points out that quite commonly it means "and yet," and sometimes marks so definite a contrast that its sense becomes "but" rather than "and." For example, in Matt. xxiii. 3, "they say *and* do not," the "and" is clearly equivalent to "but." In Matt. vi. 26, "Behold the birds of the heaven, that they sow not, neither do they reap, nor gather into barns; *and* your heavenly Father feedeth them" the "and" might well be translated "and yet." So in vii. 29, the verse we are now considering, "yet" brings out the meaning better than "and." "For he taught them as one having authority, yet not as their scribes." The multitudes were astonished at his teaching, for he taught as one having a scribe's authority, yet his doctrine was amazingly different from that of the scribes.

To give his message as a scribe would have other advantages for our Lord. It would secure him a welcome in the Galilean synagogues, invitations to teach and preach in them, and full liberty to expound the Law. Again, he wished to gather disciples round him and to travel with them. That was a recognized and permitted custom of the scribes. But anyone else who adopted it would be exposed to constant suspicion, if not to arrest. In view of frequent local risings, the Roman officials watched anxiously any group which might prove to be the nucleus of a conspiracy. But a rabbi could travel and confer with his disciples and be free from interference of this kind. Again, when a rabbi faced an audience and sat down—the recognized signal that he proposed to teach—from him the listeners would expect instruction about religion and the Law, not a speech on political or other topics. Finally, this choice helped to solve the problem of subsistence. The more prominent rabbis were often maintained by devout women of wealth. St. Luke gives us the names of some of those who "ministered of their substance" to our Lord, providing for the simple needs of himself and his disciples. Obviously, it was a custom easily abused, and Jesus himself denounced the rabbis who "devoured widows' houses." But those whose gifts he accepted were well-to-do, and their practical aid enabled him to concentrate on his mission, instead of having to depend on manual labour for his daily food.

II

Amazingly different, then, as our Lord's teaching seemed from that which they were accustomed to hear from other rabbis, his status as a scribe does not appear to have been questioned by his listeners until a few days before the Crucifixion. Then there came a blunt challenge from the scribes—probably, as they came with the chief priests, Sadducean scribes—in Jerusalem. "You sit here as 'one having authority' to teach matters of the Law," they said in effect; "but show us your credentials. 'By what authority doest thou these things, and who gave thee this authority?'" He replied, it will be remembered, with a counter-question about the Baptist. Had not a direct commission from God made rabbinic credentials needless for him? And that question his challengers were afraid to answer, when "neither tell I you by what authority I do these things" was the reply of Jesus.

But we shall naturally ask what was the attitude of the religious leaders towards Jesus, and what was his to them? We may consider the Pharisees first, because his language about them, or some of them, has caused discussion and perplexity. Certainly he was not the personal opponent of all of them; on the contrary, he had close friends among them, and on one occasion at least a group of Pharisees delivered him from arrest by Herod's emissaries. In fact, during the earlier stages of the ministry, it seems probable that most of the Pharisees regarded Jesus as one of their own number, as a Pharisaic scribe. His beliefs in the Messianic kingdom, in angels, in the resurrection were shared by them and rejected by the Sadducees, so that at first the Pharisees would listen to him with approval, as a supporter of their distinctive doctrines against their rivals, the Sadducees. But this feeling received a severe shock when he began publicly to heal on the sabbath, and to attack the official interpretation of the sabbath-law. The orthodox Pharisee honestly believed that to violate the sabbath as Jesus did was a most flagrant sin; this for them was fundamental doctrine, taught by all their scribes, and accepted without question. Soon he showed that he attached no importance to many of their ceremonial laws, such as those about the washing of vessels; he actually claimed the power to forgive sin, he was willing to make friends of publicans and disreputable women. All this genuinely shocked the average Pharisee. Unhappily, to lead him to a wiser judgment was almost impossible, because he was completely sure that the tradition he had received, and the scribes who had taught him, were infallible. Here was the real difficulty. The code of Pharisaism was so austere that not many people would adopt it as a rule of life if their religion were at heart a mere sham. The average Pharisee did walk according to the light that was in him, but unhappily that light was darkness. His ideals, his very conception of God, were wrong, and his self-complacency, his complete assurance that the scribes were right, made him impervious to any other teaching. Therefore the dismay and even horror which many of our Lord's words and acts caused him were perfectly genuine. That Jesus was apparently a scribe, that on some points of doctrine he seemed to be an ardent defender of the Pharisaic as against the Sadducean doctrines, only increased the consternation felt by the pious Pharisee when the Law as he understood it and the Tradition were openly flouted.

The real source of this Pharisaic perversion were the rabbis or scribes. They it was who insisted on the "traditions which made the word of God of none effect," who taught their doctrines as the Pharisaic creed, who proclaimed them to the multitude as the one true form of religion, and "moved heaven and earth" to gain new adherents. They, or some of them, paraded their sanctity, "for a pretence" made long prayers, loved salutations and chief seats. They, said Jesus, would receive "greater condemnation"—greater, possibly, than the ordinary Pharisee, the rank-and-file whom they guided; condemnation would be greater for the leaders than for the led.

Every reader of the Gospels must have been impressed by that tremendous denunciation of the "scribes and Pharisees" which fills 33 verses of Matthew xxiii. With it we must compare an earlier and shorter discourse in Luke xi on the same subject, while incidental rebukes of Pharisaism are scattered over the Gospels. The almost overwhelming severity of Matt. xxiii is resented by Jewish readers. Dr. C. G. Montefiore, for instance, observed of our Lord (*The Religious Teaching of Jesus*, p. 53) that "except in the way of sheer abuse and bitter vituperation, he did nothing to win over to his own conception of religion the rabbis and Pharisees who ventured to criticize and dislike him." This is strangely to forget that the parable of the Prodigal Son was spoken in the presence of "the Pharisees and scribes" (Luke xv. 2), and that the "elder son," to whom not abuse or vituperation but most loving entreaties are addressed, is clearly meant to typify the Pharisee, with his "I never transgressed a commandment" . . . But some Christian commentators, who could not attribute "sheer abuse and bitter vituperation," to our Lord, have tried, in various strange ways, to soften down the force of his words. Dr. Oesterley, for example, (*S.P.C.K. Commentary*, N.T., p. 18), having pointed out that the Pharisees were divided into followers of the rigid Shammai tradition and of the more liberal Hillel, adds: "we may well believe, therefore, that the denunciations found in the Gospels were uttered against the Shammaite Pharisees," and no others, so that "woe unto you, scribes and Pharisees" had to be understood by the hearers in this restricted sense. Yet no hints of any such limitation is to be found in the Gospels. It seems not surprising that the editors of the *Commentary* appended a footnote to warn the reader against hasty acceptance of this view.

A less improbable explanation may be that our Lord's

severest condemnation was directed against the scribes, not the general body of Pharisees. "Woe unto you, scribes and Pharisees" no more necessarily implies that two distinct classes are addressed than would a speech which began "Soldiers and Englishmen." This might mean simply "English soldiers," as the other might mean "Pharisaic scribes." If we assume that our Lord's words were directed to a single class, the scribes— "you who are scribes and Pharisees"—we shall find that this removes a number of difficulties. For instance, the address in Matthew xxiii begins: "The scribes and Pharisees sit on Moses' seat; all things therefore whatsoever they bid you" . . . and Professor Goudge in the *S.P.C.K. Commentary* wrote: "these verses are amazing as ascribed to our Lord . . . They confuse the scribes with the Pharisees. The scribes might conceivably be regarded as the spiritual successors of Moses, but the Pharisees were a religious party without any official authority." This supposed confusion vanishes if the reference is not to two sets but to a single set of people, not to scribes and Pharisees separately, but to those who are both, the Pharisaic scribes.

In Luke xi "a Pharisee asketh him to dine with him, and he went in and sat down to meat," and during the meal our Lord is represented as uttering six "woes," three of them against Pharisees generally, and three against the scribes. As Professor Creed remarks (*Commentary on Luke*, p. 165), "there is something artificial about this arrangement," and one of the charges here brought against "the Pharisees" in general is brought against "the scribes" alone in Mark. It must seem highly improbable that Jesus, having accepted an invitation to dine with a Pharisee, would use this occasion for denouncing his host and all who shared his views as "full of extortion and wickedness." But when our Lord, as the result of this hospitable invitation, found himself dining with a group of Pharisees, he might well use this chance of warning them against the scribes who misled them. Someone immediately carried a report of this to scribes in the neighbourhood, and when our Lord left the house a number of them were waiting for him, "to catch something out of his mouth."

Speaking generally, then, while some Pharisees were his friends, while others—perhaps a considerable number—were both disturbed and influenced by his teaching, the attitude of the fraternity as a body towards him was that of shocked surprise. On some points, apparently, he was their ally and an orthodox rabbi, yet on many others he disregarded, and encouraged his hearers to disregard, what they placed among the essentials of religion. In particular, what he taught about the sabbath and fasting seemed quite outrageous. And it was impossible to know what he would say next, or when, in almost casual fashion, he would sweep aside some view which united tradition upheld. Certainly the conflict between him and their own Pharisaic scribes was acute. Yet there was no denying the power of his words, his ability to refute the scribes by skilful use of the scriptures on which they relied, his hold upon the common people of Galilee. Among the Pharisees there would have been a majority, probably, in favour of silencing Jesus as a public teacher, but hardly any desired to see him put to death.

III

Very different, and far more savage, was the attitude of the Sadducees. There is no hint that Jesus had any friends among them; indeed, he can seldom have had direct contact with them except when he was in Jerusalem. Members of the Pharisaic fraternity were to be met with in all parts of the country, and they were numerous in Galilee, but all the Sadducees, a far smaller body, seem to have had their homes in or near Jerusalem, while their leaders, the priests, with their families, spent most of their time within the Temple precincts. Yet they had their spies and emissaries in the north, and it was here that our Lord cautioned his disciples against their influence—"the leaven of the Sadducees."

Tragically misconceived as was the opposition of the Pharisees to Jesus, theirs was for the most part an entirely sincere religious opposition. In all honesty they, with few exceptions, believed that in attacking the Tradition and their interpretation of the Law Jesus was perverting the people from the way of righteousness; they condemned his doctrine as spiritually dangerous. The opposition of the Sadducees had a far lower source. From motives of self-interest they were

passionately eager to preserve the outward forms and ceremonies of Judaism, as represented by the Temple system; this
it was which gave them influence and wealth. But of real personal religion they had tragically little. So long as it did not
endanger their own position, they would not concern themselves about our Lord's teaching. If it disparaged the Traditions which the Pharisees upheld and they themselves derided,
so much the better, from the Sadducean point of view. If, on
the other hand, he said or did things likely to weaken the
Temple as a money-making business, if he tried to discredit
the established ecclesiastical position, then some means must
be found of silencing him. Above all, he must not be allowed
to promote any revolutionary movement, whether religious or
otherwise.

To understand the Gospel story it is of real importance to
keep in mind not only the antagonism between Pharisee and
Sadducee, but the character of the difference between them.
Only in a secondary sense was it religious controversy. The
primary concern of the Sadducees was with politics. The
standpoint of the Pharisees was essentially religious; it was as
a part of their religion that they looked for the coming of a
Messiah. They longed for the overthrow of the Roman power
in order that God's righteousness might be vindicated and the
supremacy of his people and their Law made clear. Some of
them, the "Zealots," wished for an armed revolt at the first
possible moment, but the source of even this desire was
religion, as they understood it. While determined to uphold
every detail of the Law and the Tradition, the Pharisees were
ready to welcome political changes; changes, they believed,
that would have a divine origin and would finally establish
their creed. In this sense, the Pharisees were religious
revolutionaries, desiring political changes for religious
reasons.

The Sadducees, on the contrary, were worldly conserva-
tives. Although most of them were priests or connected with
priestly families, the inner significance of religion meant very
little to them. The Temple was their highly lucrative business
organization. The existing state of affairs in Judaea pleased
them very well, and therefore their political policy was to
avert any change. It suited them excellently to have a Roman

governor in charge of the province, who would preserve order and keep things as they were. They had little sympathy with the wish of the Pharisees and the populace to bring about the overthrow of Roman rule. There were motives which with them counted for more than religious or patriotic fervour. As for the burden of dual taxation which was bringing the mass of their countrymen close to despair, the Sadducean hierarchy could endure this with considerable equanimity, seeing that a large portion of it—the religious dues and taxes—came into their own pockets.

In fact, then, the Sadducees were far less a religious body than a clique of wealthy and worldly politicians, desperately anxious to preserve the existing system without change, and this was the source of their increasing hostility to our Lord. If he continued to gain a popular following and, in particular, if he proclaimed himself the Messiah, public disturbances on a large scale might follow. Then, too probably, Rome would apply stern repressive measures, might enforce these indiscriminately throughout Palestine; the Temple itself, and with it the Temple system and the Sadducees, might be overturned. These fears are clearly shown in John xi. 46–48. Reports of miracles done by Jesus, and of their effect on the crowds, had been brought to members of the Sanhedrin. On this council the "chief priests" and other Sadducees still predominated, but the growing influence of the Pharisees had secured places on it for some of their rabbis, much to the annoyance of the Sadducees.

> The chief priests therefore and the Pharisees gathered a council, and said, What do we? for this man doeth many signs. If we let him thus alone, all men will believe on him: and the Romans will come and take away both our place and our nation.

which means, in effect:

> The Sadducees and Pharisees therefore held an informal meeting of the Sanhedrin, and said, What action shall we take? Undoubtedly this man is working many miracles. Unless we interfere, we shall find the masses accepting his claims. There may easily follow an armed rising against Rome, which Rome will punish by terrible reprisals, destroying both our Holy Place, the Temple, and our very existence as a nation.

"From that day forth," adds the Gospel, "they took counsel that they might put him to death." Our Lord knew well that if he went up to Jerusalem at Passover-time, and there acted and spoke in a way which would make evident his claim to be the Messiah, his arrest and condemnation by the Sanhedrin must certainly follow. But this did not turn him from his purpose. The events of Palm Sunday intensified the malignant resolve of the Sadducees. Jesus had entered the city with semi-regal pomp. In the Temple, with something of super-human force and fury, he had sent flying the traffickers and money-changers, who represented a small part of that huge system with which the Sadducean priesthood was identified. If the holy building were now a "den of thieves," the "thieves" were not only the lesser people expelled but the far more important highly-placed profiteers behind them. On Palm Sunday therefore our Lord for the first time encouraged public belief in his Messiahship and declared war upon the Sadducean organization. There followed what, humanly speaking, was the inevitable sequel. The loyal protection given by the Galileans through the daytime, the kindness of a friend, who had lent an olive-orchard where undetected and in security Jesus with his disciples could pass the nights, were alike made unavailing by the perfidy of Judas. The Sanhedrin gained its end, arrested Jesus, and prevailed upon the fears of an unhappy Roman official. Jesus of Nazareth was crucified.

The single cause of this should now be clear. It was not in the slightest degree due to any action or wish of the Jews of Palestine as a whole. Popular misunderstandings about this may have been due to the language of the Fourth Gospel. Written when the separation of Christianity from Judaism had become complete, it almost limits "the Jews" to describe the inhabitants of Judaea, and Judaea virtually meant Jerusalem. Again, as the principal inhabitants of Judaea were the members of the Sanhedrin and their associates, "the Jews" in St. John's Gospel becomes almost equivalent to "the Sanhedrin," and describes the enemies of Jesus. Thus we find: "Jesus walked in Galilee; for he would not walk in Judaea, because the Jews sought to kill him." In Jerusalem itself though some said "He is a good man," yet "no man spake of him openly, for fear of the Jews." While the feelings about Jesus in Palestine ranged from adoring love to malignant hate, there seems little doubt that to the last the great majority of those who had heard his teaching were well-disposed towards him. The Galileans gave ample proof that this was true of them. The mistake of imagining a widespread public demand for his death because a handful of hirelings in the Praetorium earned their pay by shouts of "let him be crucified" has been pointed out in the first chapter of this book. It was not, then, the weight of public opinion which caused our Lord's condemnation.

Nor was it due to the Pharisees. Many repudiated violently his doctrines, many of the rabbis were jealous of the crowds his teaching attracted, a good number of Pharisees, it must be feared, were glad rather than sorry when they heard that Jesus had been executed. Yet there were others who would disagree, and whatever Jesus had said and done, according to the Law he had not laid himself open to any capital charge. Only in an indirect way was it the religious teaching of Jesus which caused his crucifixion.

In short, the reader who studies the evidence carefully will find that the whole dreadful responsibility, apart from the weak Pilate's share, falls upon the Sanhedrin—and the Sanhedrin means the Sadducees who formed the majority of that council and controlled it. They would have little difficulty in overcoming any hesitation on the part of the few Pharisaic scribes who were among the seventy-one members. Their protests would be swept aside as, at an earlier meeting, had been that of the Pharisee Nicodemus when he pleaded tentatively on our Lord's behalf. The fact that Jesus of Nazareth was coming forward as the Messiah formed the reason why the Sadducees resolved to kill him, and it was not the religious but the political consequences of his claim which they dreaded —the probability that the claim would lead to popular demonstrations, that these demonstrations would provoke the vigorous action of Rome, that the action of Rome would mean the loss of place and power for the Sadducees themselves. It is a baseless idea that the Jews of Palestine as a body, having turned against our Lord because he disappointed their hopes, persecuted him and murdered him. The hatred and jealousy, and, even more powerfully, the self-interest and political fears of some few Sadducees, by themselves proved sufficient to effect the most awful deed in history. Many thousands of people in Palestine were deeply grieved by this tragedy, yet the merely amiable sentiments of thousands did not avert what was swiftly brought about by the hideously evil and resolute action of a very few. In this lies a warning which the human race can never afford to forget.

CHAPTER EIGHT

SOME BOOKS AND VIEWS

I

THE foregoing chapters have attempted to supply the reader with a sketch of the Gospel background, in the belief that the story of our Lord's days on earth grows more vivid and is more accurately understood when we realize something of their setting, something of the people among whom he worked, and something in their ways, thoughts, religion and problems. In proportion as we put ourselves back in that period, seeing the Palestinian Jews as he saw them, and seeing him through their eyes, we are better equipped to understand the Gospels.

But some readers may wish to fill in the picture with more detail than could be given in this small volume, or to examine for themselves the evidence on which some of its statements are based. Many points about the life and thought of the first century are still in doubt, and often in these pages I have been content to give the view which seems to me right without attempting to adduce in detail the arguments which support it or to discuss critically rival theories. To do otherwise would be to confuse the reader and to turn what aims at being a lucid and readable little book into a breathless summary or a bewildering treatise. What can be done, however, is to name some of the principal books on the New Testament age which will be useful to those with leisure for fuller study.

The literature on the subject, all of it produced within the last fifty or sixty years, is considerable. A mere list of "authorities" would fill several pages, and would be of little practical use. Even comparatively recent works, and works of indubitable value, pass out of print—through no fault of the publishers —with tragic rapidity in these times and, apart from the chance of picking up second-hand copies, become unobtainable. The reader will be best served, I think, by the mention of a few specially notable books which, in one form or another, deal with the Gospel background; books which are, or have been so well recognized as authoritative that there is a likelihood of finding them on the shelves of any good public library.

Naturally enough, many of them are the work of Jewish scholars, competent to explore and interpret the mass of rabbinical writings. In this country the pioneer among them was Alfred Edersheim. He became a Christian, at the age of twenty-one, in 1846, was afterwards ordained in the Church of England, and for many years held a small country living. After writing some preliminary studies, he produced in 1883 his *Life and Times of Jesus the Messiah*. For many years it had a considerable vogue; my copy, of 1906, is of the twelfth edition. Afterwards it was fiercely criticized, especially by writers of the Jewish faith, and for some time past has been more or less set aside as untrustworthy. Its points of weakness are obvious enough, yet they do not lessen, I think, its special value. It is unduly harsh in its judgment of Pharisaic Judaism. A convert is apt to be specially severe upon the creed he has left, and Edersheim not only trounced the Pharisees, deservedly enough, for their faults, but declined to see any of their better qualities. Again, as a study of the Gospels the book has very little value. Scholarly knowledge of the New Testament has made vast progress within the last sixty years, but even for the time at which he wrote Edersheim's exegetical and critical methods were strangely inaccurate. In fact, in no real sense was he a competent New Testament scholar. What he did know, and know with amazing thoroughness, was rabbinic literature. When he deals not with the "Life" but the "Times" of our Lord, describing Jewish customs, examining Jewish thought, showing us from first-hand examination of the records what the religious leaders of our Lord's age believed and taught, his work has a real value, and the comparative disrepute into which it has fallen is unmerited. The charge most commonly brought against him is that he fails to distinguish between different periods; that he cites, for example, rabbinical regulations of a far later date as evidence for the sabbath-keeping rules enforced in our Lord's time. Two points suggest themselves in reply. First, that arbitrary and absurd rules about Sabbath were upheld by the authorities in the Gospel period is clear from the evidence of the Gospels themselves. Secondly, the fact that rules were not reduced to a written code until a later date is no proof that only then did they come into being. On the contrary, customs and rules are apt to exist for a considerable period before being tabulated in a formal code. The fact that the rabbinic documents from which Edersheim quotes preposterous sabbatical rules are late, is no proof that the rules themselves were not in vogue much earlier, and the normal sequence of events in history suggests that they were. In short, despite its flaws, Edersheim's book still provides much interesting and authentic information to those who read it with discernment.

II

But incomparably the greatest work on our subject is Emil Schürer's *The Jewish People in the Time of Jesus Christ*, as it is entitled in the English translation. Schürer, a Jewish scholar of German nationality, was, like Edersheim, converted to Christianity. The latest edition of his book appeared, in successive volumes, between 1901 and 1909; the English translation, made from the second edition, was published in 1897. The writings of later authors have supplemented it at some points and made minor corrections at others, but none has superseded it. The five volumes—with the addition of a separate index-volume—which compose it cover the whole subject with unrivalled thoroughness, and are based upon first-hand research among early records and rabbinical treatises. It is encyclopaedic in its knowledge and completeness. The complaint that in some passages Schürer, like Edersheim, shows an anti-Pharisaic bias is probably true, yet this fault detracts little from the value of the work as a whole. The reader who does not flinch from the prospect of buying its six volumes may occasionally find them included in a second-hand catalogue at a modest price—usually between £1 and 30s. If, however, the average man tried to read through those volumes from end to end, he would speedily have to own himself defeated. The translation from the German, though competent and conscientious, is never alluring and often lamentably ponderous. Schürer is best used as an invaluable work of reference for trustworthy information on some particular point, and the full index-volume greatly assists this use. If the reader can find the work in a public library and wishes to take out a single volume, he may wisely choose the part which is labelled "Division II., Vol. II.," containing the chapters on Pharisees and Sadducees, School and Synagogue, Life under the Law, and the Messianic Hope. These are perhaps the most valuable of the whole work, and easier reading than most of the others.

Another work translated from the German is S. Schechter's *Studies in Judaism*, the two volumes of which appeared in 1896 and 1908. Only some of the essays deal with the New Testament period, but these are of high value. Dr. Thomas Walker's *The Teaching of Jesus and the Jewish Teaching of His Age* is careful and scholarly, composed to a great extent of quotations from standard authorities, both ancient and modern. Dr. Walker's acquaintance with them is extremely wide. But the work has perhaps more worth as a study of our Lord's teaching than as a help to understanding the religion and thought of his contemporaries. On this special light from a special angle is thrown by Dr. Joseph Klausner's *Jesus of Nazareth: His Life, Times, and Teaching*. Dr. Klausner, himself a Jew, wrote his book in Hebrew for his fellow-Jews. Inevitably therefore it says much from which Christians must strongly dissent, yet they will profit from learning what the orthodox Jewish standpoint is, while the information about the background of the Gospel age often supplies illuminating details not to be found elsewhere. At times, too, Dr. Klausner's admirable honesty makes him refute the allegations about Jesus by other Jewish writers. For example, on p. 255 he says:

> A theory has been put forward that Jesus never regarded himself as the Messiah and only after his death was he acclaimed as Messiah by his disciples. But had this been true it would never have occurred to his disciples (simple-minded Jews) that one who had suffered crucifixion could be the Messiah; and the messianic idea meant nothing to the Gentile converts. *Ex nihilo nihil fit:* When we see that Jesus' messianic claims became a fundamental principle of Christianity soon after his crucifixion, this is a standing proof that even in his lifetime Jesus regarded himself as the Messiah.

This, coming from the source it does, is a remarkable passage.

Few really outstanding books on the Gospel background seem to have been published between 1930 and 1940, doubtless because during this period the attention of New Testament scholars was given mainly to other departments of this subject—such, for instance, as the development of the "form-criticism" theory. But a work of great value is Dr. W. O. E. Oesterley's *The Jews and Judaism during the Greek Period*, published in 1941. It is, however, less a book to be read through than a most carefully-documented collection of records and facts; its style is not its strongest point.

Among the very numerous books dealing with some special aspect of our subject may be named *The Religion and Worship of the Synagogue*, by Dr. Oesterley and Canon Box; *The Pharisees*, by C. Herford, and *The Economic Background of the Gospels*, by Dr. F. C. Grant, of Kenyon College, Gambier, Ohio, published in 1926. Dr. W. K. Lowther Clarke's *New Testament Problems* includes (pp. 109–112) an interesting criticism of Dr. Grant's book, which, however, does not seem seriously to weaken its conclusions. To allege that "the economic factor was uppermost in the messianic hope" would have been an exaggeration. But Dr. Grant does not in fact seem to go beyond saying that this factor had an important influence upon the messianic hope, and there is good reason for believing this statement to be justified.

It would be easy to prolong this list, and it need not be assumed that works of real importance have been forgotten because they are unmentioned here. But the selection that has been made is probably sufficient for its purpose, and will supply any reader who wishes to carry further his study of the Gospel background with as much material as he is likely to need.

III

There remains one more point about which something should be said. In comparatively recent times attempts were made to justify a highly idealized picture of Pharisaic Judaism and the religious life of Palestine as they were in our Lord's days. A group of Jewish writers argued that the ideas accepted by Christianity through the centuries have been based on

inaccurate information, that grave injustice has been done to
the Pharisees, who were with a few exceptions men of admirable character, that the people of Palestine whom our Lord
knew were devoted to religion as the Pharisaic teachers expounded it, that the duties and restrictions imposed by the
Law were never found burdensome, and that the official
religion produced an atmosphere of contentment and satisfac-
tion. The most prominent and persuasive of the writers sup-
porting this view was the late Dr. C. G. Montefiore. He was a
member of the "Liberal"—which is distinct from the "Orthodox"—Jewish Church. He had an intimate knowledge of
Christian literature—his *Commentary on the Synoptic Gospels*
is, in its own way, a work of permanent value—and a profound
admiration for Jesus as a merely human teacher. As a writer
on controversial subjects, Montefiore combined an air of
pellucid candour, which impressed all his readers, with a
dexterity in special pleading which they often failed to detect.
Almost any sentence in the Gospels which cannot be recon-
ciled with his views is quietly set aside, without regard to MS.
authority, as an editorial interpolation. In all sincerity, however, he believed that the old wine could be poured into new
bottles, that acceptance of the rabbinic rule of life was fully
compatible with acceptance of the teaching of Jesus.

His opinions, amplified in numerous lectures and papers,
may conveniently be examined in two of his books: *The
Religious Teaching of Jesus* (1910) and *Rabbinic Literature and
Gospel Teaching* (1930). One of his principal contentions is
that among the people of Palestine in the first century the Law
"constituted the nation's pride," that it was "a popular Law,"
that the people "did observe it and liked observing it," as a
distinction and a privilege. Hence the Pauline contrast between
the freedom of the Law of Christ and the bondage of the Law
of Moses was imaginary, and the attacks made on the Law by
Jesus—as, for example, on the sabbath-day regulations—were
arbitrary and ill-conceived. But this argument deftly blurs the
essential difference between the Law and legalism. So far from
attacking the Law, Jesus declared that he was come to fulfil it,
and not a jot or tittle of it should pass away. But to the Law,
the venerable code traditionally ascribed to Moses, had been
attached the Tradition, the amplification and interpretation

of the Law by the scribes. Indeed, the Tradition may be said virtually to have superseded the original Law; many of the scribes taught that it was the more important of the two. And it was not the Law but the Tradition, the scribes' perversion of the Law, which our Lord attacked: "ye make the Law of none effect," he said, "through your Tradition." The rules about sabbath-observance as laid down by the Law were reasonable enough and far from burdensome; the rules about sabbath-observance as detailed in the Tradition of the scribes were infinitely troublesome and often grotesque. Jesus was angered by legalism of this type, which, in the name of expounding and applying the Law, distorted it into a fundamentally different code, and then taught that precise obedience to this code was the primary essential of "righteousness," was the first duty which God required of man.

Again, Dr. Montefiore and those who share his views object strongly to our Lord's denunciation of the "scribes and Pharisees" as reported in Matthew xxiii. They complain that, while doubtless there were bad Pharisees, "the condemnation is not based on the exceptions, on the black sheep, but on the class as a whole, as if all the rabbis of the age of Jesus were hypocrites and vipers " (*Rabbinic Literature and Gospel Teaching*, p. 322). This showed his "human weakness and limitation," because for the Pharisees, "except in the way of stern rebuke and vigorous vituperation, he was no physician " (*Religious Teaching of Jesus*, pp. 53, 54). "If," pleads Dr. Montefiore, "it be once allowed (1) that it was unfair on the part of Jesus to tar all rabbis, or all the rabbis of his age, with the same brush, or (2) that he really did not do this, or (3) that he did not mean to do this, and that it is the fault of Matthew, the editor, the whole dispute would be at an end." To which it might be added with equal force that if the Sanhedrin did not condemn our Lord, or if the Crucifixion is regarded as justifiable, or if the Crucifixion is an invention of the evangelists, no reason for blaming the Sadducees would remain. But to the Christian reader at least this line of argument will hardly seem convincing.

Probably enough, in Matt. xxiii, as elsewhere in this Gospel, a number of sayings spoken at different times are grouped together as a single discourse. Probably also, as has been pointed out in an earlier chapter, the "woes" are addressed to the scribes of the Pharisees rather than to scribes and Pharisees as two separate bodies. Once more, no argument is needed to show that in a community containing, as did that of the Pharisees, several thousand members there was a mixture of good and bad individuals. But it is illogical to concentrate attention on this one chapter in Matthew as if it stood alone. The faults of the Pharisees as a class, and the stern attitude of our Lord towards those faults, are revealed on page after page of the Gospels. In spite of the good which he found in individual Pharisees, he was justified in estimating them as a body by their scribes, their accredited leaders and teachers. And by stern language alone could he hope to break down that spiritual pride, that tragically complete self-assurance, which harmed their own souls and made them dangerous to the multitudes who accepted them as models to be copied and as the authorized teachers of religion. Between his doctrine and theirs no reconciliation was possible. On the one side was the ideal of punctilious conformity with a man-made, and highly-artificial code. On the other was the ideal of the individual soul brought, by personal trust, and love and obedience, into direct relationship with God. Only this new type of "righteousness," transcending that of the Pharisaic scribes, could win for the disciple entrance into the Kingdom of God.

To estimate the general attitude of the Palestinian Jews towards the official religion of their day, we may rely upon the evidence of the Gospels and upon our knowledge of human nature and its needs. The best evidence about the Gospel background is, after all, to be found in the Gospels themselves. They show us the Pharisees and their scribes serenely complacent, assured that obedience to their Tradition represents religion at its highest. They show us the Sadducees deeply suspicious of any political change likely to diminish their resources, and, as the payments which enriched them were levied in the name of religion, hostile to any change in the religious system which enforced these payments. But we shall search the Gospels in vain for any sign that the masses of the population, especially in Galilee, "observed and liked observing," in Dr. Montefiore's phrase, the multitudinous requirements of the rabbinic code. Had Pharisaic Judaism satisfied their spiritual needs, they would not have crowded to hear the preaching of the Baptist, with its call to personal repentance. Nor, from the beginning of our Lord's ministry, would they have sought him out, even when he wished for solitude, so eager were they to learn about a religion utterly different from legalism—"a new teaching" as they rightly termed it. Even at the end, when their official Pharisaic leaders had condemned this teaching as blasphemous, when the priests and other Sadducees had given orders for his arrest, still "all the people were very attentive to hear him." Their attitude, their courageous defiance of the Temple authorities in listening to Jesus, does not suggest a populace satisfied by the official form of religion, but a soul-starved populace, hungering for that spiritual food which, as they found, Jesus of Nazareth could give and their rabbis could not.

Our knowledge of human nature confirms this interpretation of their action. These Palestinian Jews were in a restless mood, were already in serious difficulties, were beset by fears for their future. At such a time the wish for spiritual strength and inspiration grows keen. Men and women turn away despairingly from a merely external religion, from a creed of codes and ceremonies. The task of fulfilling its demands involves an immense strain and brings no comfort. Restless and ill at ease, as were those folk in Palestine, men and women in each successive time of trouble welcome the voice which brings them a new message:

Come unto me, all ye that labour and are heavy-laden, and I will give you rest. Take my yoke upon you, and learn of me, for I am meek and lowly in heart; and ye shall find rest unto your souls.

When even the fullest possible study of the Gospel background has been made, the knowedge it gives must remain very incomplete. We have far less material for realizing the daily life in Palestine in the New Testament age than we have for reconstructing the daily life of Athens or Rome during the classical periods. None the less, we may well be impressed by the similarity between some of the problems facing its primitive people in a remote past and those with which our complex civilization has still to deal. Certainly the study will increase the reverence felt for the teaching of our Lord, who never failed to sympathize with the immediate difficulties of his hearers, yet supplied also those needs of human nature which persist in every setting and through every age.